A YEAR WITH RILKE

A YEAR WITH
RILKE

Daily Readings from the Best of

RAINER MARIA RILKE

Translated and edited by
Joanna Macy *and* Anita Barrows

HarperOne
An Imprint of HarperCollinsPublishers

To Francis Macy (1927 – 2009)

Quotes from Rilke's *Book of Hours: Love Poems to God* by Rainer Maria Rilke, translated by Anita Barrows and Joanna Macy, copyright © 1996 by Anita Barrows and Joanna Macy. Used by permission of Riverhead Books, an imprint of Penguin Group (USA) Inc.

HarperCollins books may be purchased for educational, business, or sales promotional use. For information please write: Special Markets Department, HarperCollins Publishers, 10 East 53rd Street, New York, NY 10022.

HarperCollins Web site: http://www.harpercollins.com

HarperCollins®, 📚®, and HarperOne™ are
trademarks of HarperCollins Publishers

Designed by Level C

Library of Congress Cataloging-in-Publication Data
Rilke, Rainer Maria, 1875–1926.
[Selections. English. 2009]
A year with Rilke : daily readings from the best of Rainer Maria Rilke / [compiled by] Anita Barrows and Joanna Macy. — 1st ed.
p. cm.
ISBN 978-0-06-185400-2
1. Rilke, Rainer Maria, 1875–1926—Translations into English. I. Barrows, Anita.
II. Macy, Joanna, 1929– III. Title.
PT2635.I65A6 2009a
831'.912—dc22
2009026325
12 13 RRD(H) 10 9 8 7 6 5

Contents

Introduction

A *Year with Rilke* is a full, rounded basket of passages spanning
the poet's productive life. Drawn from his letters and journals as
well as his prose and especially his poetry, the days in this book bring
Rilke into our company in richly varied ways.

Celebrated as the greatest lyric poet of the twentieth century,
Rainer Maria Rilke was born to German parents in Prague in De-
cember 1875 and died in Switzerland in December 1926 at the age of
fifty-one. At twenty-three, he was already creating the poems of *The
Book of Hours*, which would first win him an appreciative audience
across Europe. This volume includes not only those early poems but
also the last sonnet he wrote, days before his death from leukemia.

The intervening decades were entirely devoted to his calling as a
poet. This central task of his life took priority over family and finan-
cial stability, to say nothing of his passionate love affairs. Driven by an
inner necessity to sustain, as best his could, a single-minded focus on
his art, Rilke sought and accepted the support of wealthy patrons. His
poems and letters originate in places as dispersed as Sweden, Trieste,
and Spain. An inveterate walker, he experienced the raw, crowded
pressures of Paris and Rome, and for the last four years of his life
took refuge in the idyllic wine country of the Valais in the upper
Rhone Valley.

The depth of Rilke's friendships with women inspired him to
explore and express his most idiosyncratic responses to existence. The
two friendships that thread most consistently through his life are with
Lou Andreas-Salomé and Clara Westhoff. Lou's involvement with

the poet survived their passionate affair that began when he, fifteen years younger, was twenty-one. She could be said to stand at the fountainhead of his oeuvre, so profound was her impact, igniting his identification with nature and his confident masculine strength as a poet. His name change from René to Rainer was at her behest.

Clara Westhoff, a gifted and committed sculptor who had studied with Rodin, was Rilke's wife and the mother of his only child, Ruth. Their domestic life together dissolved soon after Ruth's birth, as the poet recognized the impossibility of foregoing the solitude he found essential to his work. His voluminous correspondence with Clara testifies to their enduring companionship and mutual respect as artists.

Two men in particular were instrumental to Rilke's early development as a poet: the great sculptor Auguste Rodin and a virtually unknown military cadet, Franz Kappus. While serving as Rodin's secretary in Paris, exposure to the sculptor's personality and self-discipline gave Rilke a model for taking himself seriously as an artist and directing his attention to the living world around him.

Rilke never met Franz Kappus, the military student who sent him some poems seeking his advice, but Rilke's responses over a span of five years spurred his self-examination as a creative artist. These stunning reflections became *Letters to a Young Poet*, perhaps his most widely quoted work. The themes and insights they articulate remain at the core of Rilke's vision throughout his life.

We have chosen the poems and passages here for their beauty and for the love of life they convey. Our selections were also made for their relevance to our historical moment. Although Rilke lived and worked in only the first quarter of the twentieth century, his intuitions about the time in which we are now living were extraordinarily prescient. He foresaw the costs exacted by mechanization and a profit-driven economy: the moral degradation, the wasting of life, the sense of ending.

In the face of our collective condition of danger and pervasive loss, Rilke summons us to be present to our world in all its exquisite fragility. He reminds us that there is not a more important gift we can make to life on Earth. Knowing our own vulnerability is essential, both to the artist and to all who would awaken to the miracle of what is.

Rilke's grasp of the transient nature of all things is critical to his capacity to praise and to cherish. The vibrant acuity of his perception of detail—the pacing of the caged panther, the way a gazelle moves, the gesture of a beggar in the street—is ever informed by the poet's understanding of impermanence. He points out that we cannot be "used" by what is eternal if we are ourselves everlasting. Our very embodiment and the evanescent, cyclical character of all that surrounds us allow for what is infinite to express itself. Were that not so, there would be nothing but primal unity rather than the abundance that Rilke describes over and over and names "the things."

In the face of impermanence and death, it takes courage to love the things of this world and to believe that praising them is our noblest calling. Rilke's is not a conditional courage, dependent on an afterlife. Nor is it a stoic courage, keeping a stiff upper lip when shattered by loss. It is courage born of the ever-unexpected discovery that acceptance of mortality yields an expansion of being. In naming what is doomed to disappear, naming the way it keeps streaming through our hands, we can hear the song that streaming makes.

Rilke expresses his keen sensitivity to the natural world in terms of a simple and eloquent belonging, which erases the distortions that centuries of anthropocentrism have imposed upon the human mind. Escaping the traps of sentimentality or appropriation, the poet articulates a vision in harmony with what has come to be known as deep ecology, where each life form is recognized as worthy, if not sacred, in its own right. Earth's vitality takes on a noetic quality, which can inform, guide, and radically alter those able to enter it.

"If we surrendered
to Earth's intelligence
we could rise up rooted, like trees.

"Instead we entangle ourselves
in knots of our own making
and struggle, lonely and confused."

(The Book of Hours II, 16)

Given Rilke's awareness of the ecological roots of consciousness, it is not surprising that he saw the dangers inherent in what he called "the Machine." To an extent still rare among poets, he understands the toll exacted by industrial technology. The Machine, as Rilke sees it, assaults us with its clamor and takes over so much of life that we humans are diminished, robbed of our strength and our dignity. Furthermore, the poet is bold to perceive the extent to which the Machine requires and, in turn, produces massive concentrations of capital, giving unprecedented power to the abstraction we call money. The Machine gives us the illusion of control and helps us hide from our pain.

But perhaps the most distinctive aspect of Rilke's poetry resides in his fearless confrontation with the fact of suffering. His capacity to embrace the dark and to acknowledge loss brings comfort to the reader because nothing of life is left out. There is nothing that cannot be redeemed. No degree of hopelessness, such as that of prisoners, beggars, abandoned animals, or inmates of asylums, is outside the scope of the poet's respectful attention. He allows us to see that the bestowal of such pure attention is in itself a triumph of the spirit.

This quality of beholding—of taking into oneself what one beholds—is to Rilke the central task of our being. From the outset, our engagement with the world around us is presented as reciprocal.

"All becoming has needed me.
My looking ripens things
and they come toward me, to meet and be met."

(The Book of Hours I, 1)

There is a great promise in such mutuality. As Rilke's experience unfolds through the years, these encounters become increasingly transformative, almost alchemical, where each party is the agent of the other's transfiguration.

"Can you feel now how we are changing places?
My king, my king, what is heavy turns to spirit.
If we just keep hold of each other,
you grasping the young one and I the old,
we could revolve together like stars."

(David Sings before Saul, Book of Images)

Our very relationship to the living Earth, to the larger whole of which we are a part, offers, indeed, the same possibility. The poet's realization of this occurs most memorably in a kind of epiphany in the Ninth Duino Elegy. In this poem, Rilke affirms that the purpose and meaning of our existence is the transformation we can bring forth through our seeing and naming of the world.

"Earth, isn't this what you want? To arise in us, invisible?
Is it not your dream, to enter us so wholly
there's nothing left outside us to see?

What, if not transformation,
is your deepest purpose?"

(The Ninth Duino Elegy)

The quality of presence that allows such deep change to occur cannot be found amidst social duties and distractions. The reader will note in these pages the frequency of the poet's call to solitude and his emphasis on the pearl of developing our capacity to be alone so that we can more fully know what we are seeing and feeling. This solitude is not a withdrawal from the world but an occasion for utter receptivity.

Rilke would teach us to accept death as well as life, and in so doing to recognize that they belong together as two halves of the same circle: "I am not saying that we should *love* death, but that we should love life so generously, without picking and choosing, that we automatically include it (life's other half) in our love." (Letter to Countess Margot Sizzo-Noris-Crouy)

He summons us to accept our mortality and to free ourselves from compulsions to conquer or transcend it. The very fact that we are bound to die can be cause for gratitude, for it delivers us into the immediacy and fullness of life. To Rilke, Orpheus is the one who confronts death and comes back singing. His journey to reclaim his beloved becomes the journey each of us takes to embrace our finitude and, at the same time, discover our essential identity with the source of life.

"Be forever dead in Eurydice, and climb back singing.
Climb praising as you return to connection.
Here among the disappearing, in the realm of the transient,
be a ringing glass that shatters as it rings.

Be. And know as well the need to *not* be:
let that ground of all that changes
bring you to completion now."

(Sonnets to Orpheus, II, 13)

The God who figures so frequently in Rilke's work does not stand in opposition to suffering and death. Stripped of heavenly glories and hosts of angels, this God is "dark and like a web,/ a hundred roots silently drinking." The poet evokes him in images and metaphors from nature—a drifting mist, apple bark, islands on the horizon, a coastline.

"Often when I imagine you
your wholeness cascades into many shapes.
You run like a herd of luminous deer
and I am dark, I am forest.

You are a wheel at which I stand,
whose dark spokes sometimes catch me up,
revolve me nearer to the center."

(The Book of Hours I, 45)

Rilke's God is an intimate partner, beyond all dualism of matter and spirit. We see him everywhere and, in order to exist, he needs to be seen. After *The Book of Hours* and *Letters to a Young Poet*, God is infrequently named but is nonetheless affirmed explicitly and repeatedly in the creative importance Rilke assigns to the Unsayable, the Invisible. As we hearken and give expression to the unsayable and invisible dimensions within ourselves, we are, in fact, creating God. Each time we apprehend a singular detail of the world's beauty, we are building God. Hence, he is the Coming One, unfolding through us as the future unfolds.

This brave and poignant theology is reflected in Rilke's treatment of traditional religious and mythological themes. Whether inviting us into stories from the biblical and Greek mythos or presenting the figures of the Buddha or Mohammed, Rilke points to the sacred as inseparable from the relations and processes of life.

Rilke was such a keen observer of his own creative process that he could articulate, to a most unusual degree, its nature and require-ments. For Rilke, what is needed to produce a work of art is not only solitude but also a conscious transparency. The artist must stand at the threshold between the Invisible and the visible, the Unsayable and the sayable, Non-being and Being. As translators we have, from the outset of our work with *The Book of Hours*, committed ourselves to conveying the poet's native lucidity.

In pursuing that goal, we have been immeasurably aided by the way we work together. The translation of every poem and passage in this book has been a wholly collaborative adventure. Our method is dialogical: speaking the lines aloud back and forth, first in the original German and then in successive versions of their meaning and sound in English. From the time we began translating together in 1993, there has been no distinction between our roles, and the order in which our names appear is not to indicate any priority or differentiation.

Our interactive process has engendered courage in many ways. We have been able to reach together for the luminous simplicity at the heart of a given passage. And we have emboldened each other in the choices we have made about what in Rilke's opus is most relevant to readers of the twenty-first century.

We want to express our gratitude to all who made this book pos-sible, beginning with our agent, Richard Morris, who first suggested it to us. We thank our editor, Cynthia DiTiberio, for her faith in this project and her trust in our judgment. We thank Viva Barrows-

Friedman for her dedication and vigilance in accurately assembling the many ingredients of this feast we have prepared. Finally, our most profound appreciation goes to Rainer Maria Rilke, for the honing of his gifts and for his lonely devotion to the realities he allowed to speak through him. The privilege of translating his words has enriched our lives beyond all expectation.

—*Joanna Macy and Anita Barrows*

I Choose to Begin

I love all beginnings, despite their anxiousness and their uncertainty, which belong to every commencement. If I have earned a pleasure or a reward, or if I wish that something had not happened; if I doubt the worth of an experience and remain in my past—then I choose to begin at this very second.

Begin what? I begin. I have already thus begun a thousand lives.

Early Journals

Lifting My Eyes

Lifting my eyes from the book, from the tightly sequenced lines
to the full and perfect night:
Oh how like the stars my buried feelings break free,
as if a bouquet of wildflowers
had come untied:

The upswing of the light ones, the bowing sway of the heavy ones
and the delicate ones' timid curve.
Everywhere joy in relation and nowhere grasping;
world in abundance and earth enough.

Uncollected Poems

Entering

Whoever you may be: step into the evening.
Step out of the room where everything is known.
Whoever you are,
your house is the last before the far-off.
With your eyes, which are almost too tired
to free themselves from the familiar,
you slowly take one black tree
and set it against the sky: slender, alone.
And you have made a world.
It is big
and like a word, still ripening in silence.
And though your mind would fabricate its meaning,
your eyes tenderly let go of what they see.

Book of Images

—∞∞∞—

Life's Bestowal of Riches

You might notice that in some ways the effects of our winter experiences are similar. You write of a constant sense of fullness, an almost overabundance of inner being, which from the outset counterbalances and compensates all deprivations and losses that might possibly come. In the course of my work this last long winter, I have experienced a truth more completely than ever before: that life's bestowal of riches already surpasses any subsequent impoverishment. What, then, remains to be feared? Only that we might forget this! But around and within us, how much it helps to remember!

Letter to Lisa Heise
May 19, 1922

~∞~

The Impermanence We Are

It seems
our own impermanence is concealed from us.
The trees stand firm, the houses we live in
are still there. We alone
flow past it all, an exchange of air.

Everything conspires to silence us,
partly with shame,
partly with unspeakable hope.

From the Second Duino Elegy

———∞∞∞———

Our Closest Friend

Our effort, I suggest, can be dedicated to this: to assume the unity of Life and Death and let it be progressively demonstrated to us. So long as we stand in opposition to Death we will disfigure it. Believe me, my dear Countess, Death is our friend, our closest friend, perhaps the only friend who can never be misled by our ploys and vacillations. And I do not mean that in the sentimental, romantic sense of distrusting or renouncing life. Death is our friend precisely because it brings us into absolute and passionate presence with all that is here, that is natural, that is love. . . . Life always says Yes and No simultaneously. Death (I implore you to believe) is the true Yea-sayer. It stands before eternity and says only: Yes.

Letter to Countess Margot Sizzo-Noris-Crouy
Epiphany, 1923

The Vastness of Connection

Bereft of knowledge before the heavens of my life,
I stand astonished. Oh the great stars.
Their rising and their setting. How quiet.
As if I did not exist. Am I taking part? Do I discount
their pure power? Does it rule the movement
of my blood? I will yearn for no closer connections
and accustom my heart to its farthest reaches.
Better it live with the spine-chilling stars
than with the pretense of some protection hovering near.

Uncollected Poems

Balance

Oh trees of life, when is your wintertime?
We are not in balance. Not in agreement
as migrating birds are. Late and overtaken,
we hurriedly try to catch the wind
and fall into a random swamp.
To bloom and to wilt is all the same to us.
Somewhere lions still walk the earth.
As long as their majesty endures, so does their power.

From the Fourth Duino Elegy

———⊗⊗⊗———

Overflow

Thus the overflow from things
pours into you.
Just as a fountain's higher basins
spill down like strands of loosened hair
into the lowest vessel,
so streams the fullness into you,
when things and thoughts cannot contain it.

From The Book of Hours II, 10

———∞∞∞———

To Praise

Praise, my dear one.
Let us disappear into praising.
Nothing belongs to us.

Uncollected Poems
(From Elegy to Marina Tsvetayeva-Efron)

———⬦⬦⬦———

To Be in Nature Now

A solitary sojourn in the country is, especially at this moment, only half real, because the sense of harmlessness in being with nature is lost to us. The influence on us of nature's quiet, insistent presence is, from the start, overwhelmed by our knowledge of the unspeakable human fate that, night and day, irrevocably unfolds.

Letter to Lou Andreas-Salomé
September 9, 1914

—⊷⊷—

The Panther

His gaze, forever blocked by bars,
is so exhausted it takes in nothing else.
All that exists for him are a thousand bars.
Beyond the thousand bars, no world.

The strong, supple pacing
moves in narrowing circles.
It is a dance at whose center
a great will is imprisoned.

Now and again the veil over his pupils
silently lifts. An image enters,
pierces the numbness,
and dies away in his heart.

New Poems

Be Ahead of All Parting

Be ahead of all parting, as if it had already happened,
like winter, which even now is passing.
For beneath the winter is a winter so endless
that to survive it at all is a triumph of the heart.

Be forever dead in Eurydice, and climb back singing.
Climb praising as you return to connection.
Here among the disappearing, in the realm of the transient,
be a ringing glass that shatters as it rings.

Be. And know as well the need to *not* be:
let that ground of all that changes
bring you to completion now.

To all that has run its course, and to the vast unsayable
numbers of beings abounding in Nature,
add yourself gladly, and cancel the cost.

Sonnets to Orpheus II, 13

—∞∞∞—

What Lies Ahead

Nothing alien happens to us, but only what has long been our own. We have already had to rethink so many concepts about motion; now we must also begin to learn that what we call fate comes not from outside us but from within. . . . Just as for so long we were mistaken about the movement of the sun, we are still mistaken about what lies ahead of us in time.

Borgeby gärd, Sweden, August 12, 1904
Letters to a Young Poet

Through All That Happens

As you unfold as an artist, just keep on, quietly and earnestly, growing through all that happens to you. You cannot disrupt this process more violently than by looking outside yourself for answers that may only be found by attending to your innermost feeling.

Paris, February 17, 1903
Letters to a Young Poet

—⊗∞⊗—

Not by Grasping

A god can do it. But tell me how
a person can flow like that through the slender lyre.
Our mind is split. At the crossroads in our heart
stands no temple for Apollo.

Song, as you teach us, is not a grasping,
not a seeking for some final consummation.
To sing is to be. Easy for a god.
But when do *we* simply be? When do *we*

become one with earth and stars?
It is not achieved, young friend, by being in love,
however vibrant that makes your voice.

Learn to forget you sang like that. It passes.
Truly to sing takes another kind of breath.
A breath in the void. A shudder in God. A wind.

Sonnets to Orpheus I, 3

—∞∞∞—

The Lute

I am the lute. When you describe my body,
its beautiful curving lines,
speak as if speaking of a ripely
curving fruit. Exaggerate the darkness you glimpse in me.

It was Tullia's darkness, which at first was hidden
in her most secret place. The brightness of her hair
was like a sun-filled hall. At moments
some tone from within me

was reflected in her face
and she would sing to me.
Then I arched myself against her softness
and what was within me entered her at last.

New Poems

And Everything Matters

The tasks that have been entrusted to us are often difficult. Almost everything that matters is difficult, and everything matters.

Worpswede, July 16, 1903
Letters to a Young Poet

———∞∞∞———

Your Singing Continues

As swiftly as the world is changing,
like racing clouds,
all that is finished
falls home to the ancient source.

Above the change and the loss,
farther and freer,
your singing continues,
god of the lyre.

How can we embrace our sorrows
or learn how to love,
or see what we lose

when we die? Only your song
over the earth
honors our life and makes it holy.

Sonnets to Orpheus I, 19

God Speaks

I am, you anxious one.

Don't you sense me, ready to break
into being at your touch?
My murmurings surround you like shadowy wings.
Can't you see me standing before you
cloaked in stillness?
Hasn't my longing ripened in you
from the beginning
as fruit ripens on a branch?

I am the dream you are dreaming.
When you want to awaken, I am waiting.
I grow strong in the beauty you behold.
And with the silence of stars I enfold
your cities made by time.

The Book of Hours I, 19

~∞~

The Man Watching (II)

What we triumph over is so small,
and the victory makes us small too.
The eternal and uncommon
refuses to be bent by us.
Like the angel who appeared
to the wrestler in the Old Testament:
when his opponent's sinews
grow hard as metal in the struggle,
they feel to his fingers like strings
on which to play a depthless melody.

Whoever is conquered by this angel
when the angel does not refuse to fight
walks away erect and ennobled,
strengthened by that fierce hand
that, like a sculptor's, shaped him.
Winning does not tempt that man.
His growth is this: to be defeated
by ever greater forces.

Book of Images

If I Cried Out

If I cried out, who
in the hierarchies of angels
would hear me?

And if one of them should suddenly
take me to his heart,
I would perish in the power of his being.
For beauty is but the beginning of terror.
We can barely endure it
and are awed
when it declines to destroy us.

From the First Duino Elegy

———⊗⊗⊗———

Sing, My Heart

Sing, my heart, the gardens you never walked,
like gardens sealed in glass balls, unreachable.
Sing the waters and roses of Isfahan and Shiraz;
praise them, lush beyond compare.

Swear, my heart, that you will never give them up.
That the figs they ripened ripened for you.
That you could tell by its fragrance
each blossoming branch.

Don't imagine you could ever let them go
once they made the daring choice: to be!
Like a silken thread, you entered the weaving.

Whatever image you take within you deeply,
even for a moment in a lifetime of pain,
see how it reveals the whole—the great tapestry.

Sonnets to Orpheus II, 21

———∞∞∞———

A Deeper Reality

All the worlds of the universe plunge into the Invisible as into a yet deeper reality. Certain stars increase in intensity and extinguish themselves in the angels' endless awareness. Others move toward transformation slowly and with great effort, and their next self-realization occurs in fear and terror.

We are the transformers of Earth. Our whole being, and the flights and falls of our love, enable us to undertake this task.

Letter to Witold Hulewicz
November 13, 1925

~ꝏ~

The Beauty of You

In deep nights I dig for you like treasure.
For all I have seen
that clutters the surface of my world
is poor and paltry substitute
for the beauty of you
that has not happened yet. . . .

From The Book of Hours II, 34

January 26

The Great God Sleep

That great god Sleep: I yield to him all greediness for time. What does he care about Time! Ten hours, eleven, even twelve—if he wants to consume them in his silencing and privileged way, let him. Alas, I seldom manage to retire early; evening is my time to read. Seductive books, aided by the improbably intensifying noises of the old house, usually keep me awake till past midnight. The personal errands of a mouse in the thick walls of some yet-to-be-cleared inner room deepen the mystery of the endless surrounding night.

Letter to Lou Andreas-Salomé
January 13, 1923

———◆———

The Solitude We Are

To speak again of solitude, it becomes ever clearer that in truth there is nothing we can choose or avoid. We *are* solitary. We can delude ourselves and act as if this were not so. That is all we can do. How much better to realize from the start that that is what we are, and to proceed from there. It can, of course, make us dizzy, for everything our eyes rest upon will be taken from us, no longer is anything near, and what is far is endlessly far.

Borgeby gärd, Sweden, August 12, 1904
Letters to a Young Poet

Am I Not the Whole?

God, are you then the All? And I the separated one
who tumbles and rages?
Am I not the whole? Am I not all things
when I weep, and you the single one, who hears it?

From The Book of Hours *II, 3*

You Come and Go

You come and go. The doors swing closed
ever more gently, almost without a shudder.
Of all who move through the quiet houses,
you are the quietest.

We become so accustomed to you,
we no longer look up
when your shadow falls over the book we are reading
and makes it glow.

From The Book of Hours I, 45

Alone

No. Of my heart I will make a tower
and stand on its very edge,
where nothing else exists—just once again pain
and what cannot be said, and once again world.

Once again in all that vastness
now dark, now light again, the single thing I am,
one final face confronting
what can never be appeased.

That ultimate face, enduring as stone,
at one with its gravity,
drawn by distances that could dissolve it
into some promise of the sacred.

New Poems

The One Who Is Coming

Why not think of God as the one who is coming, who is moving toward us from all eternity, the Future One, culminating fruit of the tree whose leaves we are? What stops you from projecting his birth on times to come and living your life as a painful and beautiful day in the history of an immense pregnancy? Do you not see how all that is happening is ever again a new beginning? And could it not be His Beginning, for to commence is ever in itself a beautiful thing. If he is to be fulfillment, then all that is lesser must precede him, so that he can fashion himself from out of the greatest abundance. Must he not be last, in order to include everything within himself? And what meaning would be ours, if he, for whom we yearn, had already existed?

Rome, December 23, 1903
Letters to a Young Poet

Go to the Limits of Your Longing

God speaks to each of us as he makes us,
then walks with us silently out of the night.

These are the words we dimly hear:

You, sent out beyond your recall,
go to the limits of your longing.
Embody me.

From The Book of Hours I, 59

———∞∞∞———

Experiencing God

In the last analysis, I have a completely indescribable passion for experiencing God, and this God is unquestionably closer to that of the Old Testament than He is to the Messiah's Gospels. I must admit that what I have most wanted in this life has been to discover within myself a temple to earth, and to dwell therein.

Letter to Rudolf Zimmerman
March 10, 1922

It Is All About Praising

It is all about praising.
Created to praise, his heart
is a winepress destined to break,
that makes for us an eternal wine.

His voice never chokes with dust
when words for the sacred come through.
All becomes vineyard. All becomes grape,
ripening in the southland of his being.

Nothing, not even the rot
in royal tombs, or the shadow cast by a god,
gives the lie to his praising.

He is ever the messenger,
venturing far through the doors of the dead,
bearing a bowl of fresh-picked fruit.

Sonnets to Orpheus I, 7

Neighbors

You, God, who live next door:
If at times, through the long night, I trouble you
with my urgent knocking—
this is why: I hear you breathe so seldom.
I know you're all alone in that room.
If you should be thirsty, there's no one
to get you a glass of water.
I wait listening, always. Just give me a sign!
I'm right here.

As it happens, the wall between us
is very thin. Why couldn't a cry
from one of us
break it down? It would crumble
easily,
it would barely make a sound.

The Book of Hours I, 6

Inside the Rose

What can enclose
this ample innerness?
So soft is this touch,
it could soothe any wound.
What skies are reflected
on the inland lake
of these open roses,
these untroubled ones?
See how loose and lax they lie,
as if an abrupt gesture
would not scatter them.
They barely keep their shape.
They fill to overflowing
with inner space, spilling out
into days that swell
and close around them
until the whole summer becomes a room,
a room in a dream.

New Poems

Unsayable

Things are not nearly so comprehensible and sayable as we are generally made to believe. Most experiences are unsayable; they come to fullness in a realm that words do not inhabit. And most unsayable of all are works of art, which—alongside our transient lives—mysteriously endure.

Paris, February 17, 1903
Letters to a Young Poet

Mineshaft

God will not let himself be lived like an easy morning.
Whoever enters that mineshaft
leaves wide-open earth behind,
crouches in tunnels to break Him loose.

Uncollected Poems

Exposed

Exposed upon the mountains of the heart. See how small over there
the last outpost of words, and higher up,
just as small, one last farmyard of feeling.
Do you recognize it? Exposed
upon the mountains of the heart. Stony ground
under the hands.

Something still blooms here, on the dumb cliff face
blooms an unconscious weed, singing.
But where is the conscious one? He who began to be conscious
now is silent, exposed upon the mountains of the heart. . . .

Uncollected Poems

Listeners at Last

Oh when, when, when will we ever have enough
of whining and defining? Haven't champions
in the weaving of words been here already?
Why keep on trying?

Are not people perpetually, over and over and over again,
assaulted by books as by buzzing alarms?
When, between two books, the quieting sky appears,
or merely a patch of earth at evening—
rejoice . . .

Louder than all the storms, louder than all the oceans,
people have been crying out:
What abundance of quietude
the Universe must yield, if we screaming humans
can hear the crickets, and if the stars
in the screamed-at ether
can appease our hearts!

Let the farthest, oldest, most ancient
ancestors speak to us!
And let us be listeners at last, humans
finally able to hear.

Uncollected Poems

The Space Within Us

The space within us reaches out, translates each thing.
For the essence of a tree to be real for you,
cast inner space around it, out of the space
that exists in you. Encircle it with restraint.
It has no borders. Only in the realm
of your renouncing can it, as tree, be known.

Uncollected Poems

If the Confident Animal

If the confident animal coming toward us
had a mind like ours,
the change in him would startle us.
But to him his own being is endless,
undefined, and without regard
for his condition: clear,
like his eyes. Where we see future,
he sees all, and himself
in all, made whole for always.

From the Eighth Duino Elegy

In the Asylum Garden

The abandoned cloister still encloses the courtyard
as if it were holy.
It remains a retreat from the world
For those who live there now.

Whatever could happen has already happened.
Now they are glad to walk the trusted paths
that draw them apart and bring them back together,
so simple and willing.

Some, on their knees beside the planted beds,
are absorbed by what they are tending.
When no one can see, there is
a secret little gesture they make.

To touch the tender early grass,
shyly to caress it.
The green is friendly and needs protection
from the rose whose red can be too fierce

and can overpower once again
what they know in their hearts to be true.
Still the inner knowledge is always there:
how good the grass is and how soft.

New Poems

The Buddha

As if he were listening: stillness, distance.
We hold our breath and cease to hear it.
He is like a star surrounded
by other stars we cannot see.

He is all things. Do we really expect him
to notice us? What need could he have?
If we prostrated ourselves at his feet,
he would remain deep and calm like a cat.

For what threw us down before him
has circled in him for millions of years.
He, who has gone beyond all we can know
and knows what we never will.

New Poems

Love Song

How shall I hold my soul
to not intrude upon yours? How shall I
lift it beyond you to other things?
I would gladly lodge it
with lost objects in the dark,
in some far still place
that does not tremble when you tremble.

But all that touches us, you and me,
plays us together, like the bow of a violin
that from two strings draws forth one voice.
On what instrument are we strung?
What musician is playing us?
Oh sweet song.

New Poems

To Darkness

You, darkness, of whom I am born—

I love you more than the flame
that limits the world
to the circle it illumines
and excludes all the rest.

But the dark embraces everything:
shapes and shadows, creatures and me,
people, nations—just as they are.

From The Book of Hours I, 11

Born of Both Worlds

Is Orpheus of this world? No. The vastness of his nature
is born of both realms.
If you know how the willow is shaped underground,
you can see it more clearly above.

We are told not to leave food
on the table overnight: it draws the dead.
But Orpheus, the conjuring one,
mixes death into all our seeing,

mixes it with everything.
The wafting of smoke and incense
is as real to him as the most solid thing.

Nothing can sully what he beholds.
He praises the ring, the bracelet, the pitcher,
whether it comes from a bedroom or a grave.

Sonnets to Orpheus I, 6

Prayer

Night, so still,
where things entirely white
and things of red and all colors of the rainbow
are lifted into the one stillness
of one darkness—
bring me as well
to immersion in the Many.

Is my mind too taken with light?
If my face were not visible,
would I still feel separate from other things?

Look at my hands:
Don't they lie there like tools?
Doesn't the ring on that finger
look just like itself? Does not the light
lie upon them with such trust—
as if knowing they are the very same
when held in darkness.

Book of Images

Live the Questions

I want to ask you, as clearly as I can, to bear with patience all that is unresolved in your heart, and try to love the questions themselves, as if they were rooms yet to enter or books written in a foreign language. Don't dig for answers that can't be given you yet: you cannot live them now. For everything must be lived. Live the questions now, perhaps then, someday, you will gradually, without noticing, live into the answer.

Worpswede, July 16, 1903
Letters to a Young Poet

———◦◦◦———

There Is No Image

I want to utter you. I want to portray you
not with lapis or gold, but with colors made of apple bark.
There is no image I could invent
that your presence would not eclipse.

From The Book of Hours I, 60

What Is Within You

Think, dear sir, of the world you carry within you . . . be it remembrance of your own childhood or longing for your own future. Only be attentive to what is arising in you, and prize it above all that you perceive around you. What happens most deeply inside you is worthy of your whole love. Work with that and don't waste too much time and courage explaining it to other people.

Rome, December 23, 1903
Letters to a Young Poet

To Trust Our Sadness

Consider whether great changes have not happened deep inside your being in times when you were sad. The only sadnesses that are unhealthy and dangerous are those we carry around in public in order to drown them out. Like illnesses that are treated superficially, they only recede for a while and then break out more severely. Untreated they gather strength inside us and become the rejected, lost, and unlived life that we may die of. If only we could see a little farther than our knowledge reaches and a little beyond the borders of our intuition, we might perhaps bear our sorrows more trustingly than we do our joys. For they are the moments when something new enters us, something unknown. Our feelings grow mute in shy embarrassment, they take a step back, a stillness arises, and the new thing, which no one knows, stands in the midst of it all and says nothing.

Borgeby gärd, Sweden, August 12, 1904
Letters to a Young Poet

—⊗∞⊗—

Knots of Our Own Making

How surely gravity's law,
strong as an ocean current,
takes hold of even the smallest thing
and pulls it toward the heart of the world.

Each thing—
each stone, blossom, child—
is held in place.
Only we, in our arrogance,
push out beyond what we each belong to
for some empty freedom.

If we surrendered
to earth's intelligence
we could rise up rooted, like trees.

Instead we entangle ourselves
in knots of our own making
and struggle, lonely and confused.

So, like children, we begin again
to learn from the things,
because they are in God's heart;
they have never left him.

The Book of Hours II, 16

What Links Us

Bless the spirit that makes connections,
for truly we live in what we imagine.
Clocks move alongside our real life
with steps that are ever the same.

Though we do not know our exact location,
we are held in place by what links us.
Across trackless distances
antennas sense each other.

Pure attention, the essence of the powers!
Distracted by each day's doing,
how can we hear the signals?

Even as the farmer labors
there where the seed turns into summer,
it is not his work. It is Earth who gives.

Sonnets to Orpheus I, 12

Let Life Happen to You

What should I say about your tendency to doubt your struggle or to harmonize your inner and outer life? My wish is ever strong that you find enough patience within you and enough simplicity to have faith. May you gain more and more trust in what is challenging, and confidence in the solitude you bear. Let life happen to you. Believe me: life is in the right in any case.

Furnborg, Jonsered, Sweden, November 4, 1904
Letters to a Young Poet

Parents and Children

Oh, if only our parents were born at the same moment we were, how much conflict and bitterness we would be spared. But parents and children can only go after each other—not with each other. And so an abyss lies between us, which, now and then, nothing but a little love can span.

Early Journals

What You Cannot Hold

You who let yourselves feel: enter the breathing
that is more than your own.
Let it brush your cheeks
as it divides and rejoins behind you.

Blessed ones, whole ones,
you where the heart begins:
You are the bow that shoots the arrows
and you are the target.

Fear not the pain. Let its weight fall back
into the earth;
for heavy are the mountains, heavy the seas.

The trees you planted in childhood have grown
too heavy. You cannot bring them along.
Give yourselves to the air, to what you cannot hold.

Sonnets to Orpheus I, 4

FEBRUARY 27

The Secret of Death

The great secret of death, and perhaps its deepest connection with us, is this: that, in taking from us a being we have loved and venerated, death does not wound us without, at the same time, lifting us toward a more perfect understanding of this being and of ourselves.

Letter to Countess Margot Sizzo-Noris-Crouy
January 23, 1924

The Unspeaking Center

She who reconciles the ill-matched threads
of her life, and weaves them gratefully
into a single cloth—
it's she who drives the loudmouths from the hall
and clears it for a different celebration

where the one guest is you.
In the softness of evening
it's you she receives.

You are the partner of her loneliness,
the unspeaking center of her monologues.
With each disclosure you encompass more
and she stretches beyond what limits her,
to hold you.

The Book of Hours I, 17

Change

Want the change. Be inspired by the flame
where everything shines as it disappears.
The artist, when sketching, loves nothing so much
as the curve of the body as it turns away.

What locks itself in sameness has congealed.
Is it safer to be gray and numb?
What turns hard becomes rigid
and is easily shattered.

Pour yourself out like a fountain.
Flow into the knowledge that what you are seeking
finishes often at the start, and, with ending, begins.

Every happiness is the child of a separation
it did not think it could survive. And Daphne, becoming a laurel,
dares you to become the wind.

Sonnets to Orpheus II, 12

—∞∞∞—

To the Beloved

Extinguish my eyes, I'll go on seeing you.
Seal my ears, I'll go on hearing you.
And without feet I can make my way to you,
without a mouth I can swear your name.

Break off my arms, I'll take hold of you
with my heart as with a hand.
Stop my heart, and my brain will start to beat.
And if you consume my brain with fire,
I'll feel you burn in every drop of my blood.

The Book of Hours II, 7

Not Prisoners

If we imagine our being as a room of any size, it seems that most of us know only a single corner of that room, a spot by the window, a narrow strip on which we keep walking back and forth. That gives a kind of security. But isn't insecurity with all its dangers so much more human?

We are not prisoners of that room.

Borgeby gärd, Sweden, August 12, 1904
Letters to a Young Poet

To Love

To love does not mean to surrender, dissolve, and merge with another person. It is the noble opportunity for an individual to ripen, to become something in and of himself. To become a world in response to another is a great immodest challenge that has sought him out and called him forth.

Rome, May 14, 1904
Letters to a Young Poet

—⚬⚬⚬—

In Our Own Way

Ever turned toward what we create, we see in it
only reflections of the Open, darkened by us.
Except when an animal silently looks us through and through.
This is our fate: to stand
in our own way. Forever
in the way.

From the Eighth Duino Elegy

Where I Am Going

Again the murmur of my own deep life grows stronger,
flowing along wider shores.
Things grow ever more related to me,
and I see farther into their forms.
I become more trustful of the nameless.
My mind, like a bird,
rises from the oak tree into the wind,
and my heart sinks through the pond's reflected day
to where the fishes move.

Book of Images

As the Century Ends

I'm living just as the century ends.

A great leaf, that God and you and I
have covered with writing
turns now, overhead, in strange hands.
We feel the sweep of it like a wind.

We see the brightness of a new page
where everything yet can happen.

Unmoved by us, the fates take its measure
and look at one another, saying nothing.

The Book of Hours I, 8

MARCH 8

— ⋘ —

A New Clarity

Allow your judgments their own undisturbed development, which, like any unfolding, must come from within and can by nothing be forced or hastened. Everything is gestation and then birth. To allow each impression and each embryo of a feeling to complete itself in the dark, in the unsayable, the not-knowing, beyond the reach of one's own understanding, and humbly and patiently to await the dawning of a new clarity: that alone is the way of the artist—in understanding as in creating.

Viareggio, April 23, 1903
Letters to a Young Poet

The Prisoner (I)

My hand has one gesture left:
to push things away.
From the rock dampness drips
on old stones.

This dripping is all I can hear.
My heart keeps pace
with the drops falling
and sinks away with them.

If the drops fell faster
an animal might come to drink.
Somewhere it is brighter than this—
but what do we know.

New Poems

The Prisoner (II)

Just imagine: what for you now is sky and wind,
air to breathe and light to see,
becomes stone right up to the little space
made by my heart and hands.

And what you now call tomorrow and
soon and next year and after that—
becomes an open wound, full of pus.
It festers and never drains.

And what has been
becomes a madness.
It rages and mocks within you,
twisting your mouth with crazed laughter.

And what had been God
becomes your jailer
and blocks with his filthy eye
your last escape.

And still you live.

New Poems

Loneliness

Loneliness is like the rain.
It rises from the sea toward evening
and from distant plains moves into sky
where it ever belongs.
And from the sky it falls upon us in the city.

It rains here below in the twilight hours
when alleyways wind toward morning
and when lovers, finding nothing,
leave the failure of each other's arms,
and when two who loathe each other
must share the same bed:

Then loneliness flows with the rivers. . . .

Book of Images

The Loner

Like one who has traveled distant oceans
am I among those who are forever at home.
The crowded days are spread across their tables,
but to me the far-off holds more life.

Behind my face stretches a world
no more lived in, perhaps, than the moon.
But the others leave no feeling alone
and all their words are inhabited.

The things I brought back with me
seem strange here and out of place.
In their own land they moved like animals,
but here they hold their breath in shame.

Book of Images

I Opened Myself

I opened myself too wide. I forgot
there's more outside than things and animals
at ease with themselves, whose eyes reflect
the wholeness of their lives.
I forgot my habit of grasping every look
that fell on me: looks, opinions, scrutiny.

Uncollected Poems

Praise the World

Praise the world to the angel: leave the unsayable aside.
Your exalted feelings do not move him.
In the universe he inhabits you are a novice.
Therefore show him what is ordinary, what has been
shaped from generation to generation, shaped by hand and eye.
Tell him of things. He will stand still in astonishment,
the way you stood by the ropemaker in Rome
or beside the potter on the Nile.
Show him how happy a thing can be, how innocent and ours,
how even a lament takes pure form,
serves as a thing, dies as a thing,
while a violin, blessing it, fades.

And the things, even as they pass,
understand that we praise them.
Transient, they are trusting us
to save them—us, the most transient of all.
As if they wanted in our invisible hearts
to be transformed
into—oh, endlessly—into us.

From the Ninth Duino Elegy

—∞∞∞—

In the Madhouse

They are quiet now. The walls
inside their minds have fallen.
The hours of understanding
draw near and soon will pass.

Sometimes at night, watching at the window,
it is suddenly all right.
What their hands touch is solid,
and their hearts lift as if in prayer.
Their eyes gaze, relieved,

upon the garden
at last undeformed, and safely
contained within its square,
which in contrast to the uneasy world
keeps being itself and never gets lost.

New Poems

───∞∞───

Love the Solitude

Much that may one day be possible can already be prepared by the solitary individual, and built with his own hands which make fewer mistakes. Therefore love your solitude and bear the pain of it without self-pity. The distance you feel from those around you should trouble you no more than your distance from the farthest stars. Be glad that you are growing, and realize that you cannot take anyone with you; be gentle with those who stay behind. Be confident and calm before them, and don't torment them with your doubts or distress them with your ambitions which they wouldn't be able to comprehend. Find in a true and simple way what you have in common with them, which does not need to change when you yourself change and change again. When you see them, love life in a form that is not your own, and be kind to all the people who are afraid of their aloneness.

Worpswede, July 16, 1903
Letters to a Young Poet

The Pieces of My Shame

In alleyways I sweep myself up
out of garbage and broken glass.
With my half-mouth I stammer you,
who are eternal in your symmetry.
I lift to you my half-hands
in wordless beseeching, that I may find again
the eyes with which I once beheld you.

I am a city by the sea
sinking into a toxic tide.
I am strange to myself, as though someone unknown
had poisoned my mother as she carried me.

It's here in all the pieces of my shame
that now I find myself again.

From The Book of Hours II, 2

—❦—

The Interior Castle

Nowhere, Beloved, will the world exist, but within us.
Our lives are constant transformations. The external
grows ever smaller. Where a solid house once stood,
now a mental image takes its place,
almost as if it were all in the imagination.
Our era has created vast reservoirs of power,
as formless as the currents of energy they transmit.
Temples are no longer known. In our hearts
these can be secretly saved. Where one survives—
a Thing once prayed to, worshipped, knelt before—
its true nature seems already to have passed
into the Invisible. Many no longer take it for real,
and do not seize the chance to build it
inwardly, and yet more vividly, with all its pillars and statues.

From the Seventh Duino Elegy

Like a Web

When I lean over the chasm of myself—
it seems
my God is dark
and like a web: a hundred roots
silently drinking.

This is the ferment I grow out of.

From The Book of Hours I, 3

—∞∞∞—

Coming to Be

From infinite longings
finite deeds arise . . .

But in these dancing tears,
what is often withheld can be found:
our strength.

Book of Images

———⊗⊗⊗———

Spring!

Spring! And Earth is like a child
who has learned many poems by heart.
For the trouble of that long learning
she wins the prize.

Her teacher was strict. We loved the white
of the old man's beard. Now we can ask her
the many names of green, of blue,
and she knows them, she knows them!

Earth, school is out now. You're free
to play with the children. We'll catch you,
joyous Earth. The happiest will catch you!

All that the teacher taught her—the many thoughts
pressed now into roots and long
tough stems: she sings! She sings!

Sonnets to Orpheus I, 21

Since I've Learned to Be Silent

Since I've learned to be silent, everything has come so much closer to me. I am thinking of a summer on the Baltic when I was a child: how talkative I was to sea and forest; how, filled with an unaccustomed exuberance, I tried to leap over all limits with the hasty excitement of my words. And how, as I had to take my leave on a morning in September, I saw that we never give utterance to what is final and most blessed, and that all my rhapsodic Table d'hote conversations did not approach either my inchoate feelings or the ocean's eternal self-revelation.

Early Journals

What Will You Do, God?

What will you do, God, when I die?

I am your pitcher (when I shatter?)
I am your drink (when I go bitter?)
I, your garment; I, your craft.
Without me what reason have you?

Without me what house
where intimate words await you?
I, velvet sandal that falls from your foot.
I, cloak dropping from your shoulder.

What will you do, God? It troubles me.

From The Book of Hours I, 36

Mirrors

Any angel is frightening.
Yet, because I know of you,
I invoke you in spite of myself,
you lethal birds of the soul.

Fated to be happy from the beginning of time,
creation's spoiled immortal darlings,
summits of the cosmos shining at dawn,
pollen from heavenly blossoms, limbs of light,
hallways, stairs, thrones carved from existence,
shields of ecstasy, shrines for delight—
and suddenly, each one, *mirror*:
where our own evanescent beauty
is gathered into an enduring countenance.

From the Second Duino Elegy

———

Annunciation (I)

(The angel speaks)

It's not that you are closer to God than we;
We are all far from God.
But your hands seem to me
so wonderfully blessed,
made ready as no other woman's.
They are almost radiant.
I am the day, I am the dew.
You, though, are the tree.

I am tired now, I have traveled a long way.
Forgive me, but I have forgotten
what He, enthroned in gold like the sun,
wanted me to tell you, quiet one.
All that space made me dizzy.
but I am just the beginning.
You, though, are the tree.

Book of Images

—⊷—

Annunciation (II)

(The angel speaks)

I stretched my wings wide
and became incredibly vast.
Now your narrow dwelling
overflows with my robes.
Yet you are alone as never before,
and barely look at me.
I could be just a breeze in the grove.
You, though, are the tree.

Never was there such longing,
so great and so uncertain.
Maybe something is soon to occur
that has come to you in dreams.
I greet you, for my soul sees now
that you have ripened and are ready.
You are a high and awesome gate
and soon you will open.
You are the ear my song is seeking,
the forest in which my word is lost.

So I came and made real
what you dared so long to dream.
God looked right at me, it was blinding . . .

You, though, are the tree.

Book of Images

Remembering

And you wait. You wait for the one thing
that will change your life,
make it more than it is—
something wonderful, exceptional,
stones awakening, depths opening to you.

In the dusky bookstalls
old books glimmer gold and brown.
You think of lands you journeyed through,
of paintings and a dress once worn
by a woman you never found again.

And suddenly you know: that was enough.
You rise and there appears before you
in all its longings and hesitations
the shape of what you lived.

Book of Images

———∞∞∞———

Life's Other Half

I am not saying that we should love death, but rather that we should love life so generously, without picking and choosing, that we automatically include it (life's other half) in our love. This is what actually happens in the great expansiveness of love, which cannot be stopped or constricted. It is only because we exclude it that death becomes more and more foreign to us and, ultimately, our enemy.

It is conceivable that death is infinitely closer to us than life itself. . . . What do we know of it?

Letter to Countess Margot Sizzo-Noris-Crouy
Epiphany, 1923

—◦◦◦—

Dread and Bliss

The person who has not, in a moment of firm resolve, accepted—yes, even rejoiced in—what has struck him with terror—he has never taken possession of the full, ineffable power of our existence. He withdraws to the edge; when things play out, he will be neither alive nor dead.

To discover the unity of dread and bliss, these two faces of the same divinity (indeed, they reveal themselves as a single face that presents itself differently according to the way in which we see it): that is the essential meaning and theme of both my books (*The Sonnets to Orpheus* and *The Duino Elegies*).

Letter to Countess Margot Sizzo-Noris-Crouy
April 12, 1923

The Last Supper

They are assembled around him, troubled and confused.
He seems withdrawn,
as if, strangely, he were flowing past
those to whom he had belonged.
The old aloneness comes over him.
It had prepared him for his deep work.
Now once again he will go out to the olive groves.
Now those who love him will flee from him.

He had bid them come to this last meal.
Their hands on the bread
tremble now at the words he speaks,
tremble in sudden silence
as a forest does when a gun is fired.
They long to leave, and they will.
But they will find him everywhere.

Book of Images

The Olive Grove (I)

He went out under the grey leaves,
all grey and indistinct, this olive grove,
and buried his dusty face
in the dust of his hot hands.

It has come to this. Is this how it ends?
Must I continue when I'm going blind?
Why do you want me to say you exist
when I no longer find you myself?

I cannot find you any more. Not within me.
Not in others. Not in these stones.
I find you no longer. I am alone.

I am alone with everyone's sorrow,
the sorrow I tried to relieve through you,
you who do not exist. O unspeakable shame.
Later they would say an angel came.

New Poems

The Olive Grove (II)

They would say an angel came.

Why angel? What came was night,
moving indifferently amidst the trees.
The disciples stirred in their dreams.
Why an angel? What came was night.

The night that came was like any other,
dogs sleeping, stones lying there—
like any night of grief,
to be survived till morning comes.

Angels do not answer prayers like that,
nor do they let eternity break through.
Nothing protects those who lose themselves.

New Poems

To Make Sense of Things

I yearn for my work, because it always helps me make sense of things. For never was a horror experienced without an angel stepping in from the opposite direction to witness it with me.

Letter to Marianne von Goldschmidt Rothschild
December 5, 1914

———∞∞∞———

Shining in the Distance

Already my gaze is upon the hill, the sunlit one.
The way to it, barely begun, lies ahead.
So we are grasped by what we have not grasped,
full of promise, shining in the distance.

It changes us, even if we do not reach it,
into something we barely sense, but are;
a movement beckons, answering our movement . . .
But we just feel the wind against us.

Uncollected Poems

—❧—

Threshold of Spring

Harshness gone. All at once caring spreads over
the naked gray of the meadows.
Tiny rivulets sing in different voices.
A softness, as if from everywhere,

is touching the earth.
Paths appear across the land and beckon.
Surprised once again you sense
its coming in the empty tree.

Uncollected Poems

Narcissus

Narcissus vanished. All that remained
was the fragrance of his beauty—
constant and sweet, the scent of heliotrope.
His task was only to behold himself.

Whatever emanated from him he loved back into himself.
He no longer drifted in the open wind,
but enclosed himself in a narrowing circle
and there, in its grip, he extinguished himself.

Uncollected Poems

A New Place

How delicious it is to wake up in a place where no one, no one in the world, guesses where you are. Sometimes I have stopped spontaneously in towns along my way only to taste the delight that no living being can imagine me there. How much that added to the lightness of my soul!

I remember certain days in Cordova where I lived as if transparent, because I was completely unknown. The sweetness of staying in a little Spanish town, if only to relate to certain dogs and a blind beggar —more dangerous, that blind man, because he can read you. But three days later, if he hears you come back toward his church at the same hour, he counts you now as someone who henceforth exists, and he incorporates you into his world of sound.

And there you are, destined to new birth, mystical and nocturnal.

Letter to a friend
February 3, 1923

Solitude Will Be a Support

It is good that you are about to enter a profession [the military] that will make you self-sufficient and set you on your own feet. Wait patiently to see if your inner life narrows in the grip of this profession. I consider it to be a very difficult and challenging one, for it is greatly burdened with conventions and allows little room for personal interpretations of its duties. But in the midst of these very unfamiliar conditions your inner solitude will be a support and a home to you. It will be the starting point of all your journeys.

Worpswede, July 16, 1903
Letters to a Young Poet

———✸———

How to Bloom

*The almond trees in bloom: all we can accomplish here is to ever know
ourselves in our earthly appearance.*

I endlessly marvel at you, blissful ones—at your demeanor,
the way you bear your vanishing adornment with timeless purpose.
Ah, to understand how to bloom: then would the heart be carried
beyond all milder dangers, to be consoled in the great one.

Uncollected Poems

From Their Listening, a Temple

A tree rose there. What pure arising.
Oh, Orpheus sings! Now I can hear the tree.
Then all went silent. But even in the silence
was signal, beginning, change.

Out of the stillness of the unbound forest,
animals came forth from dens and nests.
And it was not fear or cunning
that made them be so quiet,

but the desire to listen. Every cry, howl, roar
was stilled inside them. And where
not even a hut stood

or the scantest shelter
to contain their ineffable longing,
you made them, from their listening, a temple.

Sonnets to Orpheus I, 1

———∞∞———

Woman in Love

There is my window.
I awoke just now so gently, I thought I was floating off.
How far does my life extend
and where does night begin?

I could believe that everything
surrounding me is I,
transparent as a crystal,
dark and still as a crystal's depths.

I could contain within me
all the stars; so vast
is my heart, so gladly
it let him go again, the one

I have perhaps begun to love,
perhaps to hold.
Strange and unimagined,
my fate turns toward me.

What am I? Set down
like this in such immensity,
fragrant as a meadow,
moved by each passing breeze.

Calling out, yet fearful
that my call will be heard,
and destined to be drowned
in another's life.

New Poems

The Future Enters Us

It seems to me that all our sadnesses are moments of tension that we feel as paralysis because we can no longer experience our banished feelings. Because we are alone with the unfamiliar presence that has entered us, because we feel momentarily abandoned by what we've believed and grown accustomed to; because we can't keep standing as the ground shifts under our feet. That is why the sadness passes over like a wave. The new presence inside us, that which has come to us, has entered our heart, has found its way to its innermost chamber, and is no longer even there—it is already in our blood. And we don't know what it was. We could easily be persuaded that nothing happened, and yet something has changed inside us, as a house changes when a guest comes into it. We cannot say who has entered, we may never know, but there are many indications that the future enters us in just this way, to transform itself within us long before it happens. That is why it is so important to be alone and attentive when you are sad: because the seemingly uneventful and motionless moment when our future steps into us is so much closer to life than any loud and accidental point of time which occurs, as it were, from the outside.

Borgeby gärd, Sweden, August 12, 1904
Letters to a Young Poet

Spanish Trilogy (I)

From these clouds, that carelessly cover
the star that just was there—
from these mountains over there, now, for a while,
taken by the night—
from this river on the valley floor,
that glimmers with the sky's broken light—
from me and all of this: to make one thing.

From me and from the feel of the flock
brought back to the fold, to outlast
the great dark closing down of the world—
from me and from each flicker of light
from the shadowed houses—God, to make one thing.

From the strangers, among whom I know not one, God,
and from me, from me—
to make one thing. From all the slumbering ones,
coughing old men in the hospice,
sleep-drunken children in crowded beds,
from me and all I don't know,
to make the thing, oh God, God, that thing,
that, half-heaven, half-earth, gathers into its gravity
only the sum of flight,
weighing nothing but arrival.

Uncollected Poems

—◦◦◦—

Spanish Trilogy (II)

How is it that people go around
and pick up random things
and carry them about? Like the porter
who heaves market baskets from stall to stall
as they keep filling up, and he lugs his burden
and never asks, Sir, for whom is this feast?

How is it that one just stands here, like that shepherd,
so exposed to the energies of the universe,
so integral to the streaming events of space
that simply leaning against a tree in the landscape
gives him his destiny; he need do nothing more.
And yet he lacks in his restless gaze
the tranquil solace of the herd,
has nothing but world, world, each time he looks up,
world in each downward glance.

Uncollected Poems

Spanish Trilogy (III)

When I re-enter, alone, the city's crush
and its chaos of noise
and the fury of traffic surrounds me,
may I, above that hammering confusion,
remember sky and the mountain slopes
where the herds are still descending homeward.

May my courage be like those rocks
and the shepherd's daylong work seem possible to me—
the way he drifts and darkens, and with a well-aimed stone
hems in his flock where it unravels.
With slow and steady strides, his posture is pensive
and, as he stands there, noble. Even now a god might
secretly slip into this form and not be diminished.

In turn, he lingers and moves on like the day itself,
and cloud shadows pass through him, as though all of space
were thinking slow thoughts for him.

Uncollected Poems

—∞∞∞—

Survival of the Soul

What more can we accomplish now than the survival of the soul. Harm and decay are not more present than before, perhaps, only more apparent, more visible and measurable. For the harm which humanity has lived daily since the beginning cannot be increased. But there is increasing insight into humanity's capacity for unspeakable harm, and perhaps where it leads. So much in collapse, so much seeking new ways out. Room for what new can happen.

Letter to Karl and Elisabeth von der Heydt
November 6, 1914

In the Drawing Room

They are all around us, these lordly men
in courtiers' attire and ruffled shirts
like an evening sky that gradually
loses its light to the constellations; and these ladies,
delicate, fragile, enlarged by their dresses,
one hand poised on the neck-ribbon of their lapdog.
They are close to each of us, next to the reader,
beside us as we gaze at the objets d'art
they left behind, yet still possess.

Tactful, they leave us undisturbed
to live life as we grasp it
and as they could never comprehend it.
They wanted to bloom
and to bloom is to be beautiful.
But we want to ripen,
and for that we open ourselves to darkness and travail.

New Poems

Ever Again

Ever again, though we've learned the landscape of love
and the lament in the churchyard's names
and the terrible, silent abyss where the others have fallen;
ever again we walk out, two together,
under the ancient trees, ever again find a place
among wildflowers, under heaven's gaze.

Uncollected Poems

—∞∞∞—

The Joys of Travel

Oh, the joys of travel! To feel the excitement of sudden departure, not always knowing whither. Surely you and I are in agreement about that. How often did my life seem concentrated in that single moment of departure. To travel far, far—and that first morning's awakening under a new sky! And to find oneself in it—no, to discover more of oneself there. To experience there, too, where one has never been before, one's own continuity of being and, at the same time, to feel that something in your heart, somehow indigenous to this new land, is coming to life from the moment of your arrival. You feel your blood infused with some new intelligence, wondrously nourished by things you had no way of knowing.

Letter to a friend
February 3, 1923

Leda

When the god in his urgency assumed its form,
he was startled by the beauty of the swan,
so swiftly did he disappear within it.
But his deception drove him to act

before he could feel
what this unknown body was like.
The woman recognized who was upon her
and already knew what he demanded,

and what she, confused in her resistance,
could no longer withhold. His weight bearing down,
his long neck thrusting her hand aside,

the god released himself into his beloved.
Only then did he delight in his feathers
and, in that moment, become truly a swan.

New Poems

Springtimes Have Needed You

Springtimes have needed you.
And there are stars expecting you to notice them.
From out of the past, a wave rises to meet you
the way the strains of a violin
come through an open window
just as you walk by.

As if it were all by design.
But are you the one designing it?

From the First Duino Elegy

———⁂———

We, When We Feel, Evaporate

We, when we feel, evaporate.
We breathe ourselves out and gone.
Like the glow of an ember,
the fragrance we give off grows weaker.
One could well say to us,
"You have entered my blood,
this room, this springtime is full of you. . . ."
What use is that when he cannot hold us
and we disappear into him and around him?

From the Second Duino Elegy

APRIL 22

With Silence or a Solitary Joy

Just as bees gather honey, so we collect from all that happens what is sweetest—and we build Him. Even with the littlest, most insignificant thing, when it comes from love, we begin. We begin with effort and the repose that follows effort, with silence or a solitary joy, with everything we do alone without anyone to join or help us, we begin Him whom we will not live to see, any more than our ancestors could experience us. Yet they are in us, those long departed ones, they are in our inclinations, our moral burdens, our pulsing blood, and in gestures that arise from the depths of time.

Rome, December 23, 1903
Letters to a Young Poet

—◦◦◦◦◦—

It Will Reveal Itself

Seek the inner depth of things, and when they lead you to the edge
of a great discovery, discern whether it arises from a necessity of your
being. Either this discovery will strike you as superficial and you will
shed it, or it will reveal itself as intrinsic to you and grow into a strong
and honest tool of your art.

Viareggio, April 5, 1903
Letters to a Young Poet

———

Hours of Childhood

. . . Oh hours of childhood,
when each figure hid more than the past
and no future existed.
We were growing, of course, and we sometimes tried
to do it fast, half for the sake of those
whose grownupness was all they had.
Yet when we were by ourselves,
our play was in eternity. We dwelt
in the interval between world and toy,
that place created from the beginning of time
for the purest of actions.

From the Fourth Duino Elegy

——∞——

It Was As Though a Girl Came Forth

It was as though a girl came forth
from the marriage of song and lyre,
shining like springtime.
She became inseparable from my own hearing.

She slept in me. Everything was in her sleep:
the trees I had loved, the distances
that had opened, the meadows—
all that had ever moved me.

She slept the world. Singing god, how
have you fashioned her, that she does not long
to have once been awake? See: she took form and slept.

Where is her death? Will you discover
the answer before your song is spent?
If I forget her, will she disappear?

Sonnets to Orpheus I, 2

———— ⁂ ————

Your First Word Was Light

Your first word of all was *light*,
and time began. Then for long you were silent.

You second word was *man*, and fear began,
which grips us still.

Are you about to speak again?
I don't want your third word.

From The Book of Hours I, 44

Birdsong

Birds begin their calls to praise.
And they are right. We stop and listen.
(We, behind masks and in costumes!)
What are they saying? A little report,

a little sorrow and a lot of promise
that chips away at the half-locked future.
And in between we can hear the silence
they break—now healing to our ears.

Uncollected Poems

Being Ephemeral

Does Time, as it passes, really destroy?
It may rip the fortress from its rock;
but can this heart, that belongs to God,
be torn from Him by circumstance?

Are we as fearfully fragile
as Fate would have us believe?
Can we ever be severed
from childhood's deep promise?

Ah, the knowledge of impermanence
that haunts our days
is their very fragrance.

We in our striving think we should last forever,
but could we be used by the Divine
if we were not ephemeral?

Sonnets to Orpheus II, 27

Impermanence

Impermanence plunges us into the depth of all Being. And so all forms of the present are not to be taken and bound in time, but held in a larger context of meaning in which we participate. I don't mean this in a Christian sense (from which I ever more passionately distance myself) but in a sheer earthly, deep earthly, sacred earthly consciousness: that what we see here and now is to bring us into a wider—indeed, the very widest—dimension. Not in an afterlife whose shadow darkens the earth, but in a whole that is the whole.

Letter to Witold Hulewicz
November 13, 1925

The Donor

This is what he had ordered from the painters' guild.
It's not that the savior himself had appeared to him,
or even that one single bishop
ever stood beside him, as depicted here,
gently laying his hand upon him.

But this, perhaps, was all he wanted:
to kneel like this.
He had known the desire to kneel,
to hold his own outward thrusting
tightly in the heart,
the way one grasps the reins of horses.

So that when the Immense might happen,
unpromised and unpaid for,
we might hope that it wouldn't notice us
and thus, undistracted, deeply centered,
it would come closer, would come right up to us.

New Poems

———⊷⊶⊷———

Tell Me, Orpheus

Tell me, Orpheus, what offering can I make
to you, who taught the creatures how to listen?
I remember a spring day in Russia;
it was evening, and a horse . . .

He came up from the village, a gray horse, alone.
With a hobble attached to one leg
he headed to the fields for the night.
How the thick mane beat against his neck

in rhythm with his high spirits
and his impeded, lurching gallop.
How all that was horse in him quickened.

He embraced the distances as if he could sing them,
as if your songs were completed in him.
His image is my offering.

Sonnets to Orpheus I, 20

———⊗⊗⊗———

Widening Circles

I live my life in widening circles
that reach out across the world.
I may not complete this last one
but I give myself to it.

I circle around God, around the primordial tower.
I've been circling for thousands of years
and I still don't know: am I a falcon,
a storm, or a great song?

The Book of Hours I, 2

—∞∞∞—

The Scale of the Heart

To take things seriously—as my books are said to do—betokens no heaviness of spirit. Taking things seriously is no more than according things their true weight and seeing their innate value. It springs from a desire to weigh things on the scale of the heart rather than indulging in suspicion and distrust.

Letter to Rudolf Bodlander
March 13, 1922

Drudgery

I know that your profession is difficult and contrary to your nature. I cannot remove your distress; I can only urge you to consider whether all occupations are not challenging and hostile in some measure to one's individuality, and saturated with the resentments of those who grimly and sullenly pursue them from duty only. The situation in which you must live now is not more burdened with conventions, prejudices, and errors than any other—and even if some occupation appears to offer greater freedom, it is a rare person who is able to stay open to the great matters that shape authentic living. Only the person who accepts solitude can place himself under the deep laws of the universe. When he steps into the fresh morning or out into the event-filled evening, all that is not him falls away, as if he had died, although he stands in the teeming midst of life.

Rome, December 23, 1903
Letters to a Young Poet

———⊗⊗⊗———

A Circle

Surely our heart travels not only from the ghostly to the holy, but it makes a circle. And we know only half of it.

Letter to Marianne von Goldschmidt-Rothschild
December 5, 1914

The Departure of the Prodigal Son

To go forth now
from all the entanglement
that is ours and yet not ours,
that, like the water in an old well,
reflects us in fragments, distorts what we are.

From all that clings like burrs and brambles—
to go forth
and see for once, close up, afresh,
what we had ceased to see—
so familiar it had become.
To glimpse how vast and how impersonal
is the suffering that filled your childhood.

Yes, to go forth, hand pulling away from hand.
Go forth to what? To uncertainty,
to a country with no connections to us
and indifferent to the dramas of our life.

What drives you to go forth? Impatience, instinct,
a dark need, the incapacity to understand.

To bow to all this.
To let go—
even if you have to die alone.

Is this the start of a new life?

New Poems

Lovers

Lovers, you who are for a while
sufficient to each other,
help me understand who we are.
You hold each other. Have you proof?
See, my hands hold each other too.
I put my used-up face in them.
It helps me feel known.
Just from that, can we believe we endure?
You, however, who increase
through each other's delight,
you who ripen in each other's hands
like grapes in a vintage year:
I'm asking you
who we are.

You touch one another so reverently;
as though your caresses
could keep each place they cover
from disappearing. As though, underneath, you could sense
that which will always exist.
So, as you embrace, you promise each other eternity.

From the Second Duino Elegy

I Love the Dark Hours

I love the dark hours of my being.
My mind deepens into them.
There I can find, as in old letters,
the days of my life, already lived,
and held like a legend, and understood.

Then the knowing comes: I can open
to another life that's wide and timeless.

From The Book of Hours I, 5

Palm of the Hand

Hand's inner self. Sole, that does its walking
just with feelings. That holds itself face up
and, as in a mirror,
receives from heaven its own meandering pathways.
That has learned to walk on water
when it splashes.
That walks on wells,
transforming every journey.
That finds itself in other hands
and turns them into landscapes,
wanders and arrives in them,
fills them with arrival.

Uncollected Poems

—∞∞∞—

Gravity

Center, how from all things
you gather yourself. Even from those that fly
you take yourself back, Center, strongest one.

Those who stand can feel how gravity
plunges through them, like a drink through thirst.

Yet from the sleeper,
gravity drifts like rain
from unhurried clouds.

Uncollected Poems

Orchard and Road

In the traffic of our days
may we attend to each thing
so that patterns are revealed
amidst the offerings of chance.

All things want to be heard,
so let us listen to what they say.
In the end we will hear what we are:
the orchard or the road leading past.

Collected French Poems

———∞∞∞———

In Florence

I have visited the works of art at length in Florence. For hours at a time I have sat before a particular painting and shaped my opinion of it, and then later compared it to Burckhardt's fine judgments. And look: my opinion was like that of so many others.

Once, studying Botticelli's *Magnificat*, I forgot any judgment of my own or of others. That is when it happened: I recognized a battle and was awarded a victory. And my joy was like no other.

Early Journals

Things Intimate and Indifferent

For our ancestors, a house, a fountain, even clothing, a coat, was much more intimate. Each thing, almost, was a vessel in which what was human found and defined itself.

Now, from America, empty, indifferent things sweep in—pretend things, life-traps. . . . A house, in the American sense, an American apple, a grapevine, bears no relation to the hope and contemplation with which our ancestors informed and beheld them.

Letter to Witold Hulewicz
November 13, 1925

———∞∞∞———

God's True Cloak

We must not portray you in king's robes,
you drifting mist that brought forth the morning.

From The Book of Hours I, 4

Offering

. . . Our loving is not, like the flowers', the offering
of a single year. When we love, there rises in us
a sap from time immemorial. Oh my dear girl,
it is this: that we loved, in each other, not an individual
or one coming toward us, but brimming multitudes;
not a single child but the fathers
fallen to the depths of us like crumbled mountains,
and the dry riverbeds of ancestral mothers;
the whole soundless landscape
under the clear or clouded sky of fate:
all this, my dear, came before you.

From the Third Duino Elegy

—∞∞∞—

If Only for Once

If only for once it were still.
If the *not quite right* and the *why this*
could be muted, and the neighbor's laughter,
and the static my senses make—
if all of it didn't keep me from coming awake—

Then in one vast thousandfold thought
I could think you up to where thinking ends.

I could possess you,
even for the brevity of a smile,
to offer you
to all that lives,
in gladness.

The Book of Hours I, 7

——⸰⸰⸰——

Brother Body

(in the sanitarium, in Rilke's final illness)

Brother body is poor . . . that means we must be rich for him.
He was often the rich one; so may he be forgiven
for the meanness of his wretched moments.
Then, when he acts as though he barely knows us,
may he be gently reminded of all that has been shared.

Of course, we are not one but two solitaries:
our consciousness and he.
But how much we have to thank each other for,
as friends do! And illness reminds us:
friendship demands a lot.

Uncollected Poems

A Hunger Drives Us

A hunger drives us.
We want to contain it all in our naked hands,
our brimming senses, our speechless hearts.
We want to become it, or offer it—but to whom?
We could hold it forever—but, after all,
what can we keep? Not the beholding,
so slow to learn. Not anything that has happened here.
Nothing. There are the hurts. And, always, the hardships.
And there's the long knowing of love—all of it
unsayable. Later, amidst the stars, we will see:
these are better unsaid.

From the Ninth Duino Elegy

MAY 19

Nothing to Frighten Us

We are not prisoners. No traps or snares are set around us; there is nothing that should frighten or torment us. We have been put into life as into the element we most accord with, and we have, moreover, through millennia of adaptation, come to resemble this life so greatly, that we, when we hold still, through a happy mimicry, can hardly be distinguished from everything that surrounds us.

Borgeby gärd, Sweden, August 12, 1904
Letters to a Young Poet

Never Yet Spoken

I believe in all that has never yet been spoken.
I want to free what waits within me
so that what no one has dared to wish for
may for once spring clear
without my contriving.

From The Book of Hours I, 12

———— ∞∞∞ ————

Go into Yourself

There is only one thing to do. Go into yourself. Examine your reason for writing. Discover whether it is rooted in the depths of your heart, and find out whether you would rather die than be forbidden to write. Above all, ask yourself in the stillest hour of the night, have I no choice but to write? Dig deep within for the truest answer, and if this answer is a strong and simple *yes,* then build your life upon this necessity. Your life henceforth, down to its most ordinary and insignificant moment, must prove and reveal this truth.

Paris, February 17, 1903
Letters to a Young Poet

———∞∞———

Is It Not Time

Is it not time
to free ourselves from the beloved
even as we, trembling, endure the loving?
As the arrow endures the bowstring's tension
so that, released, it travels farther.
For there is nowhere to remain.

From the First Duino Elegy

———∽———

The Buddha in Glory

Center of all centers, innermost core,
almond sweetening in its self-embrace—
all of this, out to the stars,
is the fruit of your body. We greet you.

You feel how little clings to you now.
Endlessness is your shell,
and there, too, the strength.
It is summoned by the radiance

of the full and glowing suns
that wheel around you.
Yet those stars will be outlasted
by what you have begun.

New Poems

About Feelings

All feelings that gather you up and lift you are pure. If they twist and tear at your being, they are not. All tenderness you may feel for your childhood is good. Every emotion that makes more of you than you have ever been, even in your best hours, is good. Every intensification is good, if it seizes you entire and is not an intoxication or delusion, but a joy you can see into, clear to the bottom. Do you understand what I mean?

Furnborg, Jonsered, Sweden, November 4, 1904
Letters to a Young Poet

The Beggars

The shapeless heaps turn out to be beggars.
They reveal themselves as you pass by.
They are selling the nothing
their hands hold out.

New Poems

Though We Yearn

We, though we yearn for the One,
already feel the pull of other things.
Are not lovers ever pushing
at each other's limits? Lovers,
who promised each other
vastness, hunt, and home. . . .

From the Fourth Duino Elegy

———— ⸎ ————

Patience Is All

Do not measure in terms of time: one year or ten years means nothing. For the artist there is no counting or tallying up; just ripening like the tree that does not force its sap and endures the storms of spring without fearing that summer will not come. But it will come. It comes, however, only to the patient ones who stand there as if all eternity lay before them—vast, still, untroubled. I learn this every day of my life, I learn it from hardships I am grateful for: patience is all.

Viareggio, April 23, 1903
Letters to a Young Poet

—∞—

When Things Close In

It feels as though I make my own way
through massive rock
like a vein of ore
alone, encased.

I am so deep inside it
I can't see the path or any distance:
everything is close
and everything closing in on me
has turned to stone.

Since I still don't know enough about pain,
this terrible darkness makes me small.
If it's you, though—

press down hard on me, break in
that I may know the weight of your hand
and you, the fullness of my cry.

The Book of Hours III, 1

—∞—

Simply in Your Presence

I'm too alone in the world, yet not alone enough
to make each hour holy.
I'm too small in the world, yet not small enough
to be simply in your presence, like a thing—
just as it is.

From The Book of Hours I, 13

Love Between Two People

No area of human existence is so burdened with conventions as love between two people. There are life-preservers of the most varied invention, life-boats and safety vests; society has fashioned rescue strategies of every description. Since it has chosen to take love as an easy pleasure, it must make it as cheap and as safe as all public amusements should be.

Rome, May 14, 1904
Letters to a Young Poet

MAY 31

What Kind of Courage Is Required of Us?

What kind of courage is required of us?

Imagine a person taken out of his room, and without preparation or transition placed on the heights of a great mountain range. He would feel an unparalleled insecurity, an almost annihilating abandonment to the nameless. He would feel he was falling into outer space or shattering into a thousand pieces. What enormous lie would his brain concoct in order to give meaning to this and validate his senses? In such a way do all measures and distances change for the one who realizes his solitude. These changes are often sudden and, as with the person on the mountain peak, bring strange feelings and fantasies that are almost unbearable. But it is necessary for us to experience that too. We must accept our reality in all its immensity. Everything, even the unheard of, must be possible within it. This is, in the end, the only kind of courage that is required of us: the courage to meet the strangest, most awesome, and most inexplicable of phenomena.

Borgeby gärd, Sweden, August 12, 1904
Letters to a Young Poet

———∞∞∞———

Springtime People

We are no longer innocent; but we must make every effort to become primitive so that we can begin again each time, and from our hearts. We must become springtime people in order to find the summer, whose greatness we must herald.

Early Journals

Often When I Imagine You

Often when I imagine you
your wholeness cascades into many shapes.
You run like a herd of luminous deer
and I am dark, I am forest.

From The Book of Hours I, 45

——✴——

White Roses

Every day, on contemplating these exquisite white roses, I wonder if they are not the perfect image of the unity of being and non-being in our lives. That, I would say, constitutes the fundamental equation of our existence.

Letter to Madame M-R
January 4, 1923

—∞—

Wild Rosebush

How it stands there against the dark
of this late rainy hour, young and clean,
swaying its generous branches
yet absorbed in its essence as rose;
with wide-open flowers already appearing,
each unsought and each uncared-for.
So, endlessly exceeding itself
and ineffably from itself come forth,
it calls the wanderer, who in evening contemplation
passes on the road:
Oh see me standing here, see how unafraid I am
and unprotected. I have all I need.

Uncollected Poems

Lullaby

When it happens that I lose you,
will you find that you can sleep
without my whispering over you
like the rustling linden tree?

Without my lying awake beside you
and letting my words
fall upon your breast, your limbs,
your mouth, like petals of a rose?

Without my letting you be cradled
alone with what is yours,
like a garden abundant
with lavender and lemon balm.

New Poems

The Apple Orchard (I)

Come now as the sun goes down.
See how evening greens the grass.
Is it not as though we had already gathered it
and saved it up inside us,

so that now, from feelings and memories,
from new hope and old pleasures,
all mixed with inner darkness,
we fling it before us under the trees.

New Poems

The Oldest Work of Art

God is the oldest work of art. He is very poorly preserved, and many parts of Him are later additions. But that is the way things get built: by our being able to talk about Him, by our having seen everything else.

Early Journals

The Apple Orchard (II)

The trees, like those of Dürer,
bear the weight of a hundred days of labor
in their heavy, ripening fruit.
They serve with endless patience to teach

how even that which exceeds all measure
must be taken up and given away,
as we, through long years,
quietly grow toward the one thing we can be.

New Poems

———— ◦◦◦ ————

Trust

You know that the flower bends when the wind wants it to, and you must become like that—that is, filled with deep trust.

Early Journals

You Inherit the Green

And you inherit the green
of vanished gardens
and the motionless blue of fallen skies,
dew of a thousand dawns, countless summers
the suns sang, and springtimes to break your heart
like a young woman's letters.

You inherit the autumns, folded like festive clothing
in the memories of poets; and all the winters,
like abandoned fields, bequeath you their quietness.
You inherit Venice, Kazan, and Rome;

Florence will be yours, and Pisa's cathedral,
Moscow with bells like memories,
and the Troiska convent, and the monastery
whose maze of tunnels lies swallowed under Kiev's gardens.

From The Book of Hours II, 10

Earth, Isn't This What You Want

Earth, isn't this what you want? To arise in us, invisible?
Is it not your dream, to enter us so wholly
there's nothing left outside us to see?
What, if not transformation,
is your deepest purpose? Earth, my love,
I want it too. Believe me,
no more of your springtimes are needed
to win me over—even one flower
is more than enough. Before I was named
I belonged to you. I see no other law
but yours, and know I can trust
the death you will bring.

See, I live. On what?
Childhood and future are equally present.
Sheer abundance of being
floods my heart.

From the Ninth Duino Elegy

The Watchman in the Vineyards

Just as the watchman in the vineyards
has a hut, keeps vigil there,
I am that hut, Lord.
And I am night, Lord, within your night.

Wine garden, meadow, apple orchard,
field that no springtime forgets,
fig tree that yields a thousand figs
though rooted in ground as hard as marble:

fragrance exudes from your rounding branches.
You never ask if I am keeping watch.
Fearless, dissolved in juices,
your depths rise quietly around me.

The Book of Hours I, 58

The Bowl of Roses (I)

You have seen explosions of anger, seen how two boys
wrestle themselves into a single knot of hatred,
writhing on the ground like an animal assailed
by a swarm of bees. You have seen actors portray
paroxysms of rage, and maddened horses
beyond control, eyes rolling out of their heads,
teeth bared as if their very skull were shaking loose.

But now you know how things are forgotten.
For here before you stands a bowl of roses:
unforgettable, complete in itself,
a fullness of being:
self offering without surrender, sheer presence
becoming what we truly are.

New Poems

—∞∞∞—

The Bowl of Roses (II)

Soundless existence ever opening,
filling space while taking it from no one,
diminishing nothing, defined by nothing outside itself,
all coming from within, clothed in softness
and radiant in its own light, even to its outermost edge.
When have we known a thing like this,

like the tender and delicate way
that rose petal touches rose petal?
Or like this: that each petal is an eyelid,
and under it lie other eyelids
closed, as if letting all vision be cradled
in deepening sleep.

New Poems

—∞∞—

The Bowl of Roses (III)

And this above all: that through these petals
light must pass. From a thousand skies,
each drop of darkness is filtered out
and the glow at the core of each flower
grows stronger and rises into life.

And the movement of the roses
has a vibrancy none could discern,
were it not for what it ignites
in the universe entire . . .

One could say they were self-contained
if self-contained meant
to transform the world outside,
patience of springtime, guilt and restlessness,
the secrecy of fate and the darkness of Earth at evening—
on out to the streaming and fleeing of clouds
and, farther yet, the orders of the stars—
take it all and turn it into
a handful of inwardness.

See how it lies at ease in these open roses.

New Poems

—∞∞∞—

See the Flowers

See the flowers, so faithful to Earth.
We know their fate because we share it.
Were they to grieve for their wilting,
that grief would be ours to feel.

There's a lightness in things. Only *we* move forever burdened,
pressing ourselves into everything, obsessed by weight.
How strange and devouring our ways must seem
to those for whom life is enough.

If you could enter their dreaming and dream with them deeply,
you would come back different to a different day,
moving so easily from that common depth.

Or maybe just stay there: they would bloom and welcome you,
all those brothers and sisters tossing in the meadows,
and you would be one of them.

Sonnets to Orpheus II, 14

You, Orpheus

But you, divine poet, to the end a singer:
falling prey to the pack of Maenads,
you wove their shrieking into wider harmonies,
and brought from that destruction a song to build with.

No one to call when they raged and wrestled,
but the jagged stones they hurled
turned gentle when reaching you,
as if able to hear you.

Hounded by hatred, you were torn to pieces
while your music still rang amidst rocks and lions,
trees and birds. There you are singing still.

O dear lost god, you endless path!
Only because you were broken and scattered
have we become the ears of nature, and her voice.

Sonnets to Orpheus I, 26

The Animal That Never Was

This is the animal that never was.
They didn't know, and loved him anyway:
his bearing, his neck, the way he moved,
the light in his quiet eyes.

True, he didn't exist. But because they loved him
he became a real animal. They made a space for him.
And in that clear, uncluttered space, he lifted his head
and hardly needed to exist.

They fed him: not with grain, but ever
with the chance that he could be.
And that so strengthened him

that, from within, he grew a horn.
All white, he drew near to a virgin and found himself
in a silver mirror and in her.

Sonnets to Orpheus II, 4

June 19

A Wondrous Knowing of the World

Sexual pleasure is no different from the sensory experience of pure looking or the feel on the tongue of a luscious fruit; it is a wondrous knowing of the world, given to us so that we may learn its fullness and radiance. The problem is not our acceptance of it; the problem is that this experience is so often misused and squandered. It is taken to enliven the deadened places of our lives, to distract instead of heightening our awareness.

People have even made eating into something it is not meant to be. Experienced as automatic impulse on the one hand, or as excess on the other, the nature of this physical necessity is distorted, and similarly distorted are all the other simple requirements for the renewing of life.

Worpswede, July 16, 1903
Letters to a Young Poet

———⦿———

With Each Thing

Who can say what is? Who is able to judge the true worth of things?

I can only measure the world in terms of longing. All things are so ready to accommodate our many and often mistaken thoughts and wishes. With each thing I would like to rest for a night, after a day of "doing" with other things. I would like to sleep once with each thing, nestled in its warmth; to dream in the rhythm of its breathing, its dear, naked neighborliness against my limbs, and grow strong in the fragrance of its sleep. Then, early in the morning, before it awakens, before any good-byes, to move on, to move on. . . .

Early Journals

❦

Constellation

Look at the sky. Is there no constellation called Rider?
For the image is imprinted on the mind:
this arrogance made from Earth and a second one astride,
driving him and holding him back.

Hunted, then harnessed: isn't this
the sinewy nature of our being?
Path and turning, a touch to guide.
New distances. And the two are one.

But are they? Or is it only the going
that unites them? When they stop
they belong again to table or pasture.

The starry patterns fool us, too. Still,
it pleases us for a moment
to believe in them. That is all we need.

Sonnets to Orpheus I, 11

—∞∞—

I Find You There

I find you there in all these things
I care for like a brother.
A seed, you nestle in the smallest of them,
and in the huge ones spread yourself hugely.

Such is the amazing play of the powers:
they give themselves so willingly,
swelling in the roots, thinning as the trunks rise,
and in the high leaves, resurrection.

The Book of Hours I, 22

David Sings Before Saul (I)

My king, hear how my fingers on the strings
open distances we can travel through.
Stars careen around us
and we find we are falling like rain.
Earth blooms where this rain has fallen.

Girls you still remember are blooming too.
They are women now, and they draw me.
Young boys wait by the still closed door.
Slender and tense, they hold their breath.

Oh, might my playing restore it all to you!
But my music reels drunkenly.
It's those nights of yours, those nights—
my singing moves me to imagine
the exhausted forms when you had done with them.

I can accompany your memories
because I feel them. But on which strings
can I pluck for you the dark groans of your lust?

New Poems

—⊱⊰—

David Sings Before Saul (II)

My king, all of this was yours.
The force of your living
oppressed and overshadowed me.
Come down from your throne and break this harp
that you have wearied.

It is like a tree picked bare, and
through branches that once bore you fruit
a depth is staring as from days to come,
days I cannot know.

Let me sleep no more beside the harp.
Look at my hand, still a boy's hand.
Do you think it could not span
the octaves of a lover's body?

New Poems

————<small>—∞∞∞—</small>————

David Sings Before Saul (III)

Oh king, you conceal yourself in darknesses,
and yet I have you in my power.
See, nothing has stopped this song of mine.
The room grows cold around us.
My orphaned heart and your wasted one
are caught together in the blindness of your wrath,
our teeth sunk into each other,
our claws twisted in a single fist.

Can you feel now how we are changing places?
My king, my king, what is heavy turns to spirit.
If we just keep hold of each other,
you grasping the young one and I the old,
we could revolve together like stars.

New Poems

Charged with the Transfiguration of All Things

How all things are in migration! How they seek refuge in us. How each of them desires to be relieved of externality and to live again in the Beyond which we enclose and deepen within ourselves. We are convents of lived things, dreamed things, impossible things; all that is in awe of this century saves itself within us and there, on its knees, pays its debt to eternity.

Little cemeteries that we are, adorned with the flowers of our futile gestures, containing so many corpses that demand that we testify to their souls. All prickly with crosses, all covered with inscriptions, all spaded up and shaken by countless daily burials, we are charged with the transmutation, the resurrection, the transfiguration of all things. For how can we save what is visible if not by using the language of absence, of the invisible?

And how to speak this language that remains mute unless we sing it with abandon and without any insistence on being understood.

Letter to Sophy Giauque
November 26, 1925

Breath

Breath, you invisible poem!
Pure, continuous exchange
with all that is, flow and counterflow
where rhythmically I come to be.

Each time a wave that occurs just once
in a sea I discover I am.
You, innermost of oceans,
you, infinitude of space.

How many far places were once
within me. Some winds
are like my own child.

When I breathe them now, do they know me again?
Air, you silken surround,
completion and seed of my words.

Sonnets to Orpheus II, 1

Gathering God

The poets have scattered you.
A storm ripped through the stammering.
I want to gather you up again
in a vessel that makes you glad.

I wander in the thousand winds
that you are churning,
and bring back everything I find.

The blind man needed you as a cup.
The servant concealed you.
The beggar held you out as I passed.

You see, I am one who likes to look for things.

The Book of Hours I, 55

JUNE 29

Slowness

As for me, my internal pace is slow. Mine is the intrinsic slowness of the tree that embraces its growth and its blooming. Yes, I have a bit of its admirable patience. I had to train myself in it from the moment I understood the secret slowness that engenders and distills any work of art. But if I know its temporal measure, I know nothing of its immobility. Oh, the joys of travel!

Letter to a friend
February 3, 1923

I Dig for You, God, Like Treasure

My hands are bloody from digging.
I lift them, hold them open in the wind,
so they can branch like a tree.

Reaching, these hands would pull you out of the sky
as if you had shattered there,
dashed yourself to pieces in some wild impatience.

What is this I feel falling now,
falling on this parched earth,
softly,
like a spring rain?

From The Book of Hours II, 34

Sky Within Us

Oh, not to be separated,
shut off from the starry dimensions
by so thin a wall.

What is within us
if not intensified sky
traversed with birds

and deep
with winds of homecoming?

Uncollected Poems

One Sufficient Word

A rose by itself is every rose.
And this one is irreplaceable,
perfect, one sufficient word
in the context of all things.

Without what we see in her,
how can we speak our hopes
or endure a tender moment
in the winds of departure.

Les Roses
From Rilke's collected French poems

—⊗⊗⊗—

The Gift of Exploration

Dove that stayed in the open, outside the dovecote,
brought back and housed again
where neither night nor day poses danger—
she knows what protection is. . . .

The other doves not exposed to peril
do not know this tenderness.
The heart that has been fetched back can feel most at home.
Vitality is freed through what it has renounced.

Over Nothingness the universe bends.
Ah, the ball we dared to throw
fills the hands differently on its return:
it brings back the reality of its journey.

Uncollected Poems

—⟨∞⟩—

Even the Best Rulers

The tragedy of nations is perhaps this: that even the best rulers use up a piece of their people's future.

Early Journals

Gold

Gold leads a pampered life, protected by banks,
on intimate terms with the best people.
The homeless beggar is no more than a lost coin
fallen behind the bookcase or in the dustpile under the bed.

In the finest shops, money is right at home,
loving to parade itself in flowers, silk and furs.
He, the silent one, stands outside this display.
Money, near him, stops breathing.

How does his outstretched hand ever close at night?
Fate, each morning, picks it up again,
holds it out there, naked and raw.

In order to grasp what his life is like,
to see it and cherish it, you would need a song,
a song only a god could bear to hear.

Sonnets to Orpheus II, 19

Between Hammers Pounding

Between hammers pounding,
the heart exists, like the tongue
between the teeth—which still,
however, does the praising.

From the Ninth Duino Elegy

The Island (I)

The tide erases the path through the mud flats
and makes things on all sides look the same.
But the little island out there has closed its eyes.
The dike around it walls its people in.

They are as if born into a sleep
that silently blurs all destinations.
They seldom speak,
and every utterance is like an epitaph

for something cast ashore, some foreign object
that comes unexplained, and just stays.
So is everything their gaze encounters from childhood on:

not intended for them, random, unwieldy,
sent from somewhere else
to underscore their loneliness.

New Poems

━━∞━━

The Island (II)

As if lying in some crater on the moon,
each farm is encircled by its earthen banks.
And like orphans the gardens inside
are dressed and combed the same

by the storm that raises them so roughly,
scaring them all the time with threats of death.
That's when you stay indoors, gazing into
the crooked mirror at the assorted things

reflected there. Toward evening one of you
steps outside the door and draws from the harmonica
a sound as soft as weeping

such as you heard once in a distant port.
Out there, silhouetted against the sky,
one of the sheep stands motionless on the far dike.

New Poems

The Island (III)

Only what is within you is near; all else is far.
And this within: so packed and pressured,
barely contained, unsayable.
The island could be a star so insignificant

that space in its terrible blindness takes no note
and mindlessly destroys it.
Thus, unillumined and unheard,
expecting nothing

but that all this may yet come to an end,
it continues doggedly its self-invented course,
alone, outside the patterns made
by planets and the suns they orbit.

New Poems

———— ⊗⊗⊗ ————

Tanagra

A small piece of earth, burned,
as if burned by the sun's fire.
The touch of a girl's hand
seems somehow still upon it.
Feel how it remained there,
not longing for anything other,
just resting into itself
like fingers on a chin.

We take up this figure, then that,
turning them in the light.
We can almost understand
how they managed to survive.
We need only smile
and accept more fully
what it offers to our eyes.

New Poems

———∞∞∞———

Transforming Dragons

We have no reason to distrust our world, for it is not against us. If it has terrors, they are our terrors. If it has an abyss, it is ours. If dangers are there, we must try to love them. And if we would live with faith in the value of what is challenging, then what now appears to us as most alien will become our truest, most trustworthy friend. Let us not forget the ancient myths at the outset of humanity's journey, the myths about dragons that at the last moment transform into princesses. Perhaps all the dragons of our lives are princesses who are only waiting to see us act just once with beauty and courage. Perhaps every terror is, in its deepest essence, something that needs our recognition or help.

Borgeby gärd, Sweden, August 12, 1904
Letters to a Young Poet

——❧❧❧——

Continuities

Some of us have long felt continuities that have little in common with the course of history. We understand what is most distinctive in this fateful moment and what future it holds. But we, squeezed between yesterday and tomorrow, will we be mindful and receptive enough to participate in the unfolding of the larger movement?

Letter to Countess Marie von Thurn und Taxis-Hohenlohe
July 9, 1915

The Swan

This laboring of ours with all that remains undone,
as if still bound to it,
is like the lumbering gait of the swan.

And then our dying—releasing ourselves
from the very ground on which we stood—
is like the way he hesitantly lowers himself

into the water. It gently receives him,
and, gladly yielding, flows back beneath him,
as wave follows wave,
while he, now wholly serene and sure,
with regal composure,
allows himself to glide.

New Poems

━━◆◆◆━━

Some Generous Place

If I had grown in some generous place—
if my hours had opened in ease—
I would make You a lavish banquet.
My hands wouldn't clutch at You like this,
so needy and tight.

From The Book of Hours I, 21

—∞∞∞—

Bodily Delight

If only people could perceive the mystery in all life, down to the smallest thing, and open themselves to it instead of taking it for granted. If only they could revere its abundance which is undividedly both material and spiritual. For the mind's creation springs from the physical, is of one nature with it and only a lighter, more enraptured and enduring recapturing of bodily delight.

Worpswede, July 16, 1903
Letters to a Young Poet

—❧—

Who Shows a Child

Who shows a child his true world?
Who sets him among the stars, and places
in his hand the true measure of space?
Death can do this, the hugeness of death,
even before life has begun—
to hold it gently and feel no resentment,
that is enough.

From the Fourth Duino Elegy

—∞∞∞—

The Golden Hive

Nature, and the things we live with and use, precede us and come after us. But they are, so long as we are here, our possession and our friendship. They know with us our needs and our pleasures, as they did those of our ancestors, whose trusted companions they were.

So it follows that all that is here is not to be despised and put down, but, precisely because it did precede us, to be taken by us with the innermost understanding that these appearances and things must be seen and transformed.

Transformed? Yes. For our task is to take this earth so deeply and wholly into ourselves that it will resurrect within our being. We are bees of the invisible. Passionately we plunder the honey of the visible in order to gather it in the great golden hive of the invisible.

Letter to Witold Hulewicz
November 13, 1925

———◦◦◦◦———

Sometimes a Man

Sometimes a man rises from the supper table
and goes outside. And he keeps going
because somewhere to the east there's a church.
His children bless his name as if he were dead.

Another man stays at home until he dies,
stays with plates and glasses.
So then it is his children who go out
into the world, seeking the church that he forgot.

The Book of Hours II, 19

With Real Love, There Are No Recipes

Whenever people in love act out of an imagined fusion of their beings, their every action is dictated by convention. Every relation colored by such confusion is conventional, however exotic (that is, immoral) it might appear. Even separating would be a conventional step, an automatic alternative lacking in skill and creativity.

Whoever takes it seriously, discovers that, as with death which is real, so with real love, there are no easy recipes. For both these undertakings, there are no universally agreed-upon rules. But in the same measure that we begin as individuals to explore life's meaning for us, these great things come toward us to be met and known. The claims made upon us by the hard work of love are bigger than life and essential to our unfolding, and we are seldom up to them at the outset. But if we hold steady and take this love upon us as a task and a teaching, instead of losing ourselves in an easy and frivolous game behind which to hide the most honest questions of our existence—this may be felt as a small illumination and step forward by those who come long after us. That in itself would be a lot.

Rome, May 14, 1904
Letters to a Young Poet

———⚬⚬⚬———

On the Edge of Night

My room and the vastness around it,
awake in the oncoming night,
are one. I am a string
stretched taut
across resonating distances.

All things are the body of the violin,
filled with murmuring darkness.
There, grieving women lie down to dream.
There the resentments of generations
surrender to sleep . . .
A silver thread,
I reverberate:
then all that's underneath me
comes to life.

And what has lost its way
will, by my vibrant sounds,
be at last brought home
and allowed to fall endlessly
into the depthless source. . . .

Book of Images

—✕✕✕—

I Have Hymns

I have hymns you haven't heard.

There is an upward soaring
in which I bend close.
You can barely distinguish me
from the things that kneel before me.

They are like sheep, they are grazing.
I am the shepherd on the brow of the hill.
When evening draws them home
I follow after, the dark bridge thudding,

and the vapor rising from their backs
hides my own homecoming.

The Book of Hours I, 40

———∞∞∞———

Evening

Slowly evening takes on the garments
held for it by a line of ancient trees.
You look, and the world recedes from you.
Part of it moves heavenward, the rest falls away.

And you are left, belonging to neither fully,
not quite so dark as the silent house,
not quite so sure of eternity
as that shining now in the night sky, a point of light.

You are left, for reasons you can't explain,
with a life that is anxious and huge,
so that, at times confined, at times expanding,
it becomes in you now stone, now star.

Book of Images

The Lies We Tell

The lies we tell are like toys,
easy to break. Like gardens
where we play hide and seek,
and, in our excitement, make a sound
so people will know where to look.

You are the wind that catches our voice,
our own shadow grown longer.
You collection of lovely holes
in the sponge that we are.

Collected French Poems

—❧—

Fear and Fearlessness

Those who sense eternity are beyond all fear. They see in every night the place where day begins, and are consoled.

Fearlessness is necessary for summer to come. Spring can be troubled; to its blossoming, uneasiness is like a home. But fruits need the strength and calm of the sun. All must be ready to receive, with wide open gateways and substantial bridges.

A race that is born in fear comes as a stranger to the world and never finds its way home.

Early Journals

The Blessing of Earth

God, every night is hard.
Always there are some awake,
who turn, turn, and do not find you.
Don't you hear them crying out
as they go farther and farther down?
Surely you hear them weep; for they are weeping.

I seek you, because they are passing
right by my door. Whom should I turn to,
if not the one whose darkness
is darker than night, the only one
who keeps vigil with no candle,
and is not afraid—
the deep one, whose being I trust,
for it breaks through the earth into trees,
and rises,
when I bow my head,
faint as a fragrance
from the soil.

From The Book of Hours II, 3

No Worthless Place

If your daily life seems of no account, don't blame it; blame yourself that you are not poet enough to call forth its treasures. For the creative artist there is no impoverishment and no worthless place.

Paris, February 17, 1903
Letters to a Young Poet

To What Can We Turn

Oh, to what, then, can we turn
in our need?
Not to an angel. Not to a person.
Animals, perceptive as they are,
notice that we are not really at home
in this world of ours. Perhaps there is
a particular tree we see every day on the hillside,
or a street we have walked,
or the warped loyalty of habit
that does not abandon us.

Oh, and night, the night, when wind
hurls the universe at our faces.
For whom is night not there?

From the First Duino Elegy

In My Glad Hours

In my glad hours, I will make a city of your smile, a distant city that shines and lives. I will take one word of yours to be an island on which birches stand, or fir trees, quite still and ceremonial. I will receive your glance as a fountain in which things can disappear and above which the sky trembles, both eager and afraid to fall in.

I will know that all of this exists, that one can enter this city, that I have glimpsed this island and know exactly when there is no one else beside that fountain. But if I appear to hesitate, it is because I am not sure whether it is the forest through which we are walking or my own mood that is shaded and dark.

Who knows: maybe Venice, too, is just a feeling.

Early Journals

The Gazelle

(*Gazella Dorcas*)

Enchanted one: how can the harmony of two
Latin words ever attain the rhythm
that ripples through you like a promise.
From your brow rise leaf and lyre.

And all that is you turns to metaphor
in love poems whose phrases light
as rose petals remain in the expression
of one who, after reading, closes her eyes

to see you: almost in flight,
borne away in leaps that cease their springing
only when you stand stock still to listen;

as when a woman bathing in a woodland stream
pauses suddenly, and the water
mirrors her quick-turned face.

New Poems

—∞∞∞—

The Shelter of Your Heart

Who knows: eyes may be watching us
from all sides. Ah, only stumbling toward you
am I no longer on display. Growing into you,
I am forever set invisibly
in the darkening shelter of your heart.

Uncollected Poems

—∞—

Summer Fruit

Full round apple, peach, pear, blackberry.
Each speaks life and death
into the mouth. Look
at the face of a child eating them.

The tastes come from afar
and slowly grow nameless on the tongue.
Where there were words, discoveries flow,
released from within the fruit.

What we call apple—dare to say what it is,
this sweetness which first condensed itself
so that, in the tasting, it may burst forth

and be known in all its meanings
of sun and earth and here.
How immense, the act and the pleasure of it.

Sonnets to Orpheus I, 13

———⟨∞⟩———

I Come Home

I come home from the soaring
in which I lost myself.
I was song, and the refrain which is God
is still roaring in my ears.

Now I am still
and plain:
no more words.

From The Book of Hours I, 50

—∞∞—

Unafraid of What Is Difficult

Don't be confused by the nature of solitude, when something inside you wants to break free of your loneliness. This very wish, when you use it as a tool for understanding, can illumine your solitude and expand it to include all that is. Bound by conventions, people tend to reach for what is easy. It is clear, however, that here we must be unafraid of what is difficult. For all living things in nature must unfold in their particular way and become themselves at any cost and despite all opposition.

Rome, May 14, 1904
Letters to a Young Poet

———— ❊❊❊ ————

What the Things Can Teach Us

This is what the things can teach us:
to fall,
patiently to trust our heaviness.
Even a bird has to do that
before he can fly.

From The Book of Hours II, 16

Once Here

Why, then, do we have to be human
and keep running from the fate
we long for?

Oh, not because of such a thing as happiness—
that fleeting gift before loss begins.
Not from curiosity, or to exercise the heart. . . .
But because simply to be here is so much
and because what is here seems to need us,
this vanishing world that concerns us strangely—
us, the most vanishing of all. Once
for each, only once. Once and no more.
And we too: just once. Never again. But
to have lived even once,
to have been of Earth—that cannot be taken from us.

From the Ninth Duino Elegy

May What I Do Flow from Me

May what I do flow from me like a river,
no forcing and no holding back,
the way it is with children.

Then in these swelling and ebbing currents,
these deepening tides moving out, returning,
I will sing you as no one ever has,
streaming through widening channels
into the open sea.

From The Book of Hours I, 12

Try to Be Close to Things

When you feel no commonality between yourself and other people, try to be close to Things, which will not abandon you. Nights are still there and winds that blow through the trees and over many lands. Amidst the things and beings of this world so much is happening that you can take part in. And children are still the way you were as a child, that happy and that sad, and when you think of your childhood you live it again with them, the lonely childhood, and grown-ups count for nothing.

Rome, December 23, 1903
Letters to a Young Poet

———— ∞ ————

Fearful of the New

The tendency of people to be fearful of those experiences they call apparitions or assign to the "spirit world," including death, has done infinite harm to life. All these things so naturally related to us have been driven away through our daily resistance to them, to the point where our capacity to sense them has atrophied. To say nothing of God. Fear of the unexplainable has not only impoverished our inner lives, but also diminished relations between people; these have been dragged, so to speak, from the river of infinite possibilities and stuck on the dry bank where nothing happens. For it is not only sluggishness that makes human relations so unspeakably monotonous, it is the aversion to any new, unforeseen experience we are not sure we can handle.

Borgeby gärd, Sweden, August 12, 1904
Letters to a Young Poet

———⟨⟩———

The Reader

Who has not known a child like this,
who sinks into a deeper level of his being,
undisturbed by the swift turning
of each brimming page?

Even his own mother might wonder
if it is really he who sits there
saturated with his shadow.

And we, can we know
how much of him
disappears, as he reluctantly looks up
with eyes that yield
to the ready-made world without complaint?

New Poems

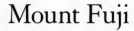

Mount Fuji

Thirty-six times and a hundred times
the artist portrayed the mountain.
Now pulled away, now compelled
(thirty-six times and a hundred times)

to return with glad impatience
to that ungraspable one.
To see it rise there, bold in outline,
withholding nothing of its majesty.

Out of each day emerging over and over,
letting the unrepeatable nights
fall away as though too small.
Each glimpse exhausted in an instant,

form ascending into form,
far off, impassive, wordless—
then suddenly the revelation
of an awareness lifting in the sky.

New Poems

Gentlest of Ways

I love you, gentlest of Ways,
who ripened us as we wrestled with you.

You, the great homesickness we could never shake off,
you, the forest that always surrounded us,

you, the song we sang in every silence,
you dark net threading through us.

You began yourself so greatly
on that day when you began us.

From The Book of Hours I, 25

---∞∞∞---

For the Sake of the Whole

Are there relations of the heart that embrace what is most cruel for the sake of wholeness? For the world is only world when everything is included.

Letter to Marianne von Goldschmidt-Rothschild
December 5, 1914

You Said "Live"

You said *live* out loud, and *die* you said lightly,
and over and over again you said *be*.

But before the first death came murder.
A fracture broke across the rings you'd ripened.
A screaming shattered the voices

that had just come together to speak you,
to make of you a bridge
over the chasm of everything.

And what they have stammered ever since
are fragments
of your ancient name.

The Book of Hours I, 9

If Something of the Ancestors Lives On

Even the next era has no right to judge anything if it lacks the ability to contemplate the past without hatred or envy. But even that judgment would be one-sided, for every subsequent era is the fruit of previous periods and carries much of the past within it. It is fortunate if something of the ancestors lives on in it and continues to be loved and protected; only then does the past become fruitful and effective.

Early Journals

I Am Sometimes Like a Tree

So I am sometimes like a tree
rustling over a gravesite
and making real the dream
of the one its living roots
embrace:

a dream once lost
among sorrows and songs.

From The Book of Hours I, 5

The Ancient Night of Your Name

A thousand theologians were immersed
in the ancient night
of your name.
Virgins awoke to you
and lads in silver shimmered
in you, you battleground.

In your cloistered walkways
poets would meet.
Gentle, deep, and masterful,
they were kings and queens of sound.

You are the tender evening hour
that all poets equally love.
You are the darkness pressing within them
and the treasure each discovers,
in surrounding you with endless praise.

A hundred thousand harps lift
and swing you out of silence.
And your primordial winds are bringing
to all things and needs
the breath of your majesty.

The Book of Hours I, 54

The Man Watching (I)

How small is what we wrestle with,
and what wrestles with us, how immense.

If we could be overcome, as things are,
in a great storm,
we would grow vast and need no names.

Book of Images

Confession

I always wish to tell someone (I don't know who) "Don't be sad." And it seems to me that this is so trusting a confession that I must express it softly and delicately and in the dimness of twilight.

Early Journals

Dread and Mystery

More than once I have mentioned to you how my life and work have been guided by the effort to overcome the old pressures that rob us of mystery, the mystery essential to our capacity to love from fullness. Humanity has been terrified and beset by dread; but is there anything noble and gracious that has not, from time to time, worn the mask of dread?

Letter to Countess Margot Sizzo-Noris-Crouy
April 12, 1923

Erect No Gravestone

Erect no gravestone. Just let the rose
bloom every year for him.
For this is Orpheus: metamorphosis
into one thing, then another.

We need not search for other names.
It is Orpheus in the singing, once and for all time.
He comes and goes. Is it not enough
that sometimes he outlasts a bowl of roses?

Oh, if you could understand—he has no choice but to disappear,
even should he long to stay. As his song
exceeds the present moment,

so is he already gone where we cannot follow.
The lyre's strings do not hold back his hands.
It is in moving farther on that he obeys.

Sonnets to Orpheus I, V

The Carousel (I)
Jardin du Luxembourg

Under its canopy, in the shade it casts,
turns a world with painted horses,
all from a land that lingers a while
before it disappears.
Some, it's true, are harnessed to a wagon,
but all have valor in their eyes.
A fierce red lion leaps among them,
and here comes 'round a snow-white elephant.

Even a stag appears, straight from the forest,
except for the saddle he wears, and,
buckled on it, a small boy in blue.

And a boy in white rides the lion,
gripping it with small clenched hands,
while the lion flashes teeth and tongue.

And here comes 'round a snow-white elephant.

And riding past on charging horses come girls,
bright-eyed, almost too old now for this children's play.
With the horses rising under them,
they are looking up and off to what awaits.

And here comes 'round a snow-white elephant.

New Poems

The Carousel (II)

It goes on and hurries to some end,
just circling and turning without a goal.
Flashes of red, of green, of grey whirl past,
solid shapes barely glimpsed.

Sometimes a smile comes toward us,
and, like a blessing, shines and is gone
in this dizzying parade with no destination.

New Poems

The Abundance of Being

In spite of Fate, the marvelous abundance
of being, like the brimming land
or like stone figures
built into gateways, bearing up balconies.

Or a bronze bell, lifting its voice
over and over against the dullness of our days.
Or that single column in Karnak, standing
long after the temple fell.

Today this extravagance flashes by
in the blur of our haste,
out of the wide yellow day into the vaulted night.

In that rush it dissolves, leaving nothing behind,
just as a plane overhead makes no mark on the sky.
Only our minds see the curve of its flight.

Sonnets to Orpheus II, 22

The Blooming of One Flower

Never, not for a single day, do we let
the space before us be so unbounded
that the blooming of one flower is forever.

From the Eighth Duino Elegy

The Knight

The knight rides forth in coal-black steel
into the teeming world.

Outside his armor everything is there: sunlight and valley,
friend and foe and feast,
May, maiden, forest and grail,
and God himself in a thousand forms
to be found along every road.

But inside the armor darkly enclosing him
crouches death. And the thought comes
and comes again:
When will the blade
pierce this iron sheath,
the undeserved and liberating blade
that will fetch me from my hiding place
where I've been so long compressed—

so that, at last, I may stretch my limbs
and hear my full voice.

Book of Images

This Press of Time

We set the pace.
But this press of time—
take it as a little thing
next to what endures.

All this hurrying
soon will be over.
Only when we tarry
do we touch the holy.

Young ones, don't waste your courage
racing so fast,
flying so high.

See how all things are at rest—
darkness and morning light,
blossom and book.

Sonnets to Orpheus I, 22

Like a Holy Face

Only as a child am I awake
and able to trust
that in every fear and every night
I will behold you again.

However often I get lost,
however far my thinking strays,
I know you will be here, right here,
untouched by time.

To me it is as if I were at once
infant, boy, man and more.
I feel that only as it circles
is abundance found.

I thank you, deep power
that works me ever more lightly
in ways I can't make out.
The day's labor grows simple now,
and like a holy face
held in my dark hands.

The Book of Hours I, 62

Fig Tree

Fig tree, for how long now have I found meaning
in the way you almost forget to bloom
and drive without drama your pure mystery
into the young determined fruit.
Like a fountain's channel your curving branches
force the sap downward and up again; look, it springs
straight from sleep into its sweetest achievement—
like the god entering a swan. . . .

From the Sixth Duino Elegy

Like a Metal That Hasn't Been Mined

You, mountain, here since mountains began,
slopes where nothing is built,
peaks that no one has named,
eternal snows littered with stars,
valleys in flower
offering fragrances of earth. . . .

Do I move inside you now?
Am I within the rock
like a metal that hasn't been mined?
Your hardness encloses me everywhere. . . .

Or is it fear
I am caught in? The tightening fear
of the swollen cities
in which I suffocate. . . .

The Book of Hours III, 2

———∞∞∞———

This Vast Landscape

Here in this vast landscape, swept by winds from the sea, I wonder if there is any person anywhere who can answer the questions that stir in the depths of your being. For even the best miss the mark when they use words for what is elusive and nearly unsayable. But nonetheless, I believe you are not left without a solution, if you turn to things like those that are refreshing my eyes. If you ally yourself with nature, with her sheer existence, with the small things that others overlook and that so suddenly can become huge and immeasurable; if you have this love for what is plain and try very simply, as one who serves, to win the confidence of what seems poor: then everything will become easier for you, more coherent and somehow more reconciling, perhaps not in your conscious mind, but in your innermost awareness.

Worpswede, July 16, 1903
Letters to a Young Poet

Not Poor

We are not poor. We are just without riches,
we who have no will, no world:
marked with the marks of the latest anxiety,
disfigured, stripped of leaves.

Around us swirls the dust of the cities,
the garbage clings to us.
We are shunned as if contaminated,
thrown away like broken pots, like bones,
like last year's calendar.

And yet if our Earth needed to
she could weave us together like roses
and make of us a garland.

For each being is cleaner than washed stones
and endlessly yours, and like an animal
who knows already in its first blind moments
its need for one thing only—

to let ourselves be poor like that—as we truly are.

The Book of Hours III, 16

The Innerness of All Things

You create yourself in ever-changing shapes
that rise from the stuff of our days—
unsung, unmourned, undescribed,
like a forest we never knew.

You are the deep innerness of all things,
the last word that can never be spoken.
To each of us you reveal yourself differently:
to the ship as a coastline, to the shore as a ship.

From The Book of Hours II, 22

Playmates

There were a few of us, playmates
in the scattered gardens of the city.
Remember how we found each other
and hesitantly liked each other,

and, like the lamb with the talking scroll,
spoke in silences. The good times we had belonged to no one.
Whose could they be? They disappeared amid all the hurrying
    people
and the worries to come with the long years.

Wagons and trucks rolled by. We didn't care.
Houses rose around us, solid but unreal, and no one knew us.
What, after all, *was* real?

Nothing. Only the ball, the beautiful arcs it made.
Not even the children were real, except for the moment
of reaching up and ah! catching the ball.

Sonnets to Orpheus II, 8

Cities

Lord, the great cities are lost and rotting.
Their time is running out. . . .
The people there live harsh and heavy,
crowded together, weary of their own routines.

Beyond them waits and breathes your earth,
but where they are it cannot reach them.

They don't know that somewhere
wind is blowing through a field of flowers.

From The Book of Hours III, 4/5

Orpheus, Eurydice, Hermes (I)

It was the mysterious mine of souls.
They threaded their way through its darkness
like veins of silver. Between roots
sprang up the blood that flows to the living
and in the dark it looked as hard as porphyry.
Nothing else was red.

Rocks were there
and forests of shadows. Bridges over chasms
and a vast, depthless lake of grey
that extended above its distant bed
like rain clouds over the land.
On either side of the pale ribbon of that one path
meadows unfolded, endlessly opening.

New Poems

Orpheus, Eurydice, Hermes (II)

On this single path they came.

First, the slender figure cloaked in blue,
looking straight ahead, tense and unspeaking.
Propelled by relentless haste,
his stride devoured the path. Under the folds
of the mantel, his hands were clenched,
and barely felt the weight of the lyre he carried with him always.
His senses were as though divided:
for his sight, like a dog, raced ahead,
turned around, came back only to run off again
and wait at the next bend.
But his hearing lingered behind.
Sometimes it seemed to be trying to reach back
to the steps of the other two
who should follow him all the way uphill.
At times there was nothing but the echo of his own footfall
and the flutter of his cloak behind him.

New Poems

—⊷⊷—

Orpheus, Eurydice, Hermes (III)

He told himself they must be coming.
He said the words aloud and heard them fade away.
They must be coming, it was just
that they were moving so quietly.
If he might turn a single time
(if to look back were not the ruin
of this whole venture now near completion),
surely he would see those two
following him so noiselessly.
The little god of journeys and messages,
winged cap above observant eyes,
wings at the ankles too, slender staff held out before him,
and entrusted to his left hand: *her.*

The one so loved, that from a single lyre
more lament came forth than from centuries' sorrows.
So loved that a world took form from that lament
where everything came to be once more:
path and village, forest and valley, field, river, animal.

And round this lamenting world, as if
it were a second earth, moved a sun and star-strewn heavens,
a grieving heaven with grief-stricken stars.
That's how loved she was.

New Poems

Orpheus, Eurydice, Hermes (IV)

Now Eurydice walked at the hand of a god,
her steps, constricted by the winding sheets,
uncertain, meek, without impatience.
She was deep within herself like a woman full with child,
and gave no thought now to the man who walked ahead
or the path that rose toward life.
She was deep within herself, and her having died
was a fullness she carried.
Like a fruit, she was filled with the sweetness
and darkness of her huge death,
still so new she could hardly grasp it.

She had entered a new virginity,
had become untouchable; her sex had closed
like a wildflower toward evening,
and her hands were so estranged from marriage
that even the god's touch, infinitely light,
disturbed her as too familiar.

New Poems

Orpheus, Eurydice, Hermes (V)

Eurydice was no longer the fair beauty
celebrated in Orpheus' singing,
no longer the fragrance and landscape of the bed,
no more the property of any man.

She was already unbound, like loosened hair,
surrendered like falling rain,
and generously offered to all creation.
She was already root.

And when, suddenly,
the god held her back and with anguish
spoke the words: *he has turned around,*
she was puzzled and softly answered, *Who?*

Up ahead, dark against the brightness of a gateway,
stood someone whose features she did not recognize.
He stood and saw how on the pale ribbon of the meadow path
the messenger god had silently turned
to watch the form of one retracing her steps,
constricted by the winding sheets,
uncertain, meek, without impatience.

New Poems

To Be Patient with Sadness

The quieter we are, the more patient and open we are in our sadnesses, the more deeply and unerringly a new revelation can enter us, and the more we can make it our own. Later on when it "happens" —when it manifests in our response to another person—we will feel it as belonging to our innermost being.

Borgeby gärd, Sweden, August 12, 1904
Letters to a Young Poet

When Doubt Serves

Doubt can serve you well, if you train it. It must become a way of knowing, a good critic. Every time doubt wants to spoil something for you, ask *why* it finds something ugly and demand proofs. Thus tested by you, doubt may become bewildered and embarrassed, even aggressive. But don't give in, demand reasons and be persistent and attentive every single time, and the day will come when, instead of a destroyer, he will become one of your best servants—perhaps one of the most intelligent of those who help you build your life.

Furnborg, Jonsered, Sweden, November 4, 1904
Letters to a Young Poet

———∞∞∞———

Fight Harmlessly

How gladly, my young friend, I would respond to your new leaflet; but here the words come hard to me. On the whole I want to acknowledge that you do well to approach this conflict as a matter intimately related to your own disposition. This is surely the most responsible attitude. You must only take care to eliminate from the tone you use all consternation and reproachfulness. My friend, this is important: fight harmlessly.

Letter to Rudolf Bodlander
March 23, 1922

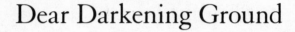

Dear Darkening Ground

Dear darkening ground,
you've endured so patiently the walls we've built,
perhaps you'll give the cities one more hour

and grant the churches and cloisters two.
And those that labor—let their work
grip them another five hours, or seven,

before you become forest again, and water, and widening wilderness
in that hour of inconceivable terror
when you take back your name
from all things.

Just give me a little more time!
I want to love the things
as no one has thought to love them,
until they're worthy of you and real.

From The Book of Hours I, 61

The Nothing You Are Grasping

Do you still not know how little endures?
Fling the nothing you are grasping
out into the spaces we breathe.
Maybe the birds
will feel in their flight
how the air has expanded.

From the First Duino Elegy

Memory Is Not Enough

To Lou Andreas-Salomé, Duino, late autumn, 1911

Memory is not enough . . .
I do not recollect. What I am
is alive in me because of you. I do not reinvent you
at sadly cooled-off places you have left behind.
Even your absence is filled
with your warmth and is more real
than your not-existing. Longing often meanders
into vagueness. Why should I throw myself away
when something in you may be
touching me, very lightly, like moonlight
on a window seat.

Uncollected Poems

Go Forth

And God said to me, Go forth:

For I am king of time.
But to you I am only the shadowy one
who knows with you your loneliness
and sees through your eyes.

He sees through my eyes
in all the ages.

From The Book of Hours I, 53

To Use Sorrow

What you say of your life—that its most painful event was also its greatest—that is, so to speak, the secret theme of these pages, indeed the inner belief that gave rise to them. It is the conviction that what is greatest in our existence, what makes it precious beyond words, has the modesty to use sorrow in order to penetrate our soul.

Letter to Madame M-R
January 4, 1923

Afternoon, Before Beethoven's *Missa Solemnis*

Let yourself not be misled by the notes
that fall to you from the generous wind.

Wait watchfully. Hands that are eternal
may come to play upon your strings.

Early Journals

Like Islands

I am learning to see something new. In addition to sky and land, a third thing has equal significance: the air.

Things usually appear to me as finite and limited in comparison with the great body of Earth. But here there are many things that seem like islands—alone, bright, caressed on all sides by ever-moving air that makes their forms stand out so clearly.

Early Journals

━━◦੦੦੦◦━━

And God Said to Me, Write:

Leave the cruelty to kings.
Without that angel barring the way to love
there would be no bridge for me
into time.

From The Book of Hours I, 53

﹡⧉﹡

Creating for Always

Those who create are like you, God.
They long for the eternal.
Carving, they say: Stone, be forever!
And that means: be yours.

And lovers also gather your inheritance.
They are the poets of one brief hour.
They kiss an expressionless mouth into a smile
as if creating it anew, more beautiful.

From The Book of Hours II, 10

The Portal (I)

They stayed right here, as if left behind
by a flood that had washed their forms
free from the rock.
The waters receding erased some details,

but their hands are generous
and grasp at nothing.
They stayed, distinguished from their native rock
only by a halo or a bishop's mitre,

and sometimes by a tranquil smile
kept alive in a face
where it lasts forever.

They retreat now into the shadowed doorway
that could be the shell of a listening ear
which captures every moan of a city in pain.

New Poems

The Portal (II)

So much life can be seen here.
Just as on a painted stage set
the world can be seen; and just as the hero
performs against this backdrop,

so here in the darkness of this portal
unfolds an eternal drama.
It is as endless and everywhere as a Father God
who wondrously transforms himself

into a Son, whose role is divided up
in many little walk-on parts,
all drawn from misery's repertoire.

For, as we know, it is only from among
the blind, the outcast, the demented,
that, as a single actor, the Savior comes forth.

New Poems

The Portal (III)

These forms loom tall, hearts restrained,
poised in eternity.
Here and there from the folds of a robe—
a gesture emerges, as formal as they,

and, arrested before completion, still is there,
overtaken by the centuries. Behold their equilibrium
as they gaze out from arches of stone
into a world they do not see.

They have not negated this world of turmoil
that bends and shakes
and still manages to hold them.

For its shapes, like acrobats,
only twist and contort themselves
so the pole on their forehead does not fall.

New Poems

The God That Is Coming

You too will find your strength.
We who must live in this time
cannot imagine how strong you will become—
how strange, how surprising,
yet familiar as yesterday.

We will sense you
like a fragrance from a nearby garden
and watch you move through our days
like a shaft of sunlight in a sickroom.

We are cradled close in your hands—
and lavishly flung forth.

From The Book of Hours II, 26

Angels

They all have tired mouths
and bright, seamless souls.
And a yearning, as for sin,
drifts at times through their dreams.

They mostly resemble each other.
In the garden of God they are silent,
like rest-notes
in his music and his might.

Only when they spread their wings,
do they stir the air—
as if God with wide sculptor's hands
were turning pages
in the hidden book of first things.

Book of Images

My Own Deep Soul

You, my own deep soul,
trust me. I will not betray you.
My blood is alive with many voices
telling me I am made of longing.

What mystery breaks over me now?
In its shadow I come into life.
For the first time I am alone with you—

you, my power to feel.

From The Book of Hours I, 39

The Violin I Keep Hearing

Strange violin, are you following me?
In how many far-off cities
has your lonely night spoken to mine?
Are hundreds playing you, or only one?

Are there, in all the great cities,
those who, without you,
would be lost in the rivers?
And why am I ever the one to hear you?

Why am I always the neighbor
to those troubled ones who force you to sing?
And to say life is harder
than the hardest of things?

Book of Images

The Books You Love

Live for awhile in the books you love. Learn from them what is worth learning, but above all love them. This love will be returned to you a thousand times over. Whatever your life may become, these books—of this I am certain—will weave through the web of your unfolding. They will be among the strongest of all threads of your experiences, disappointments, and joys.

Viareggio, April 5, 1903
Letters to a Young Poet

———— ⊸∞∞⊷ ————

In Rome

There is much beauty here, for great beauty is everywhere. Living waters flow endlessly through ancient aqueducts into the great city, and dance in many piazzas over white stone basins and spread out in spacious pools, murmuring by day and lifting their murmur into the starry, wind-softened night. There are gardens here, unforgettable boulevards, and stairs—stairs designed by Michelangelo, stairs inspired by downward flowing water—step flowing into widening step like wave into wave. From such impressions you gather yourself, you win yourself back from the clamoring multiplicity, and slowly learn to know a very few things in which the eternal is reflected, which you love and in which your solitude allows you to take part.

Rome, October 29, 1903
Letters to a Young Poet

Where Does a Smile Go

Those who are beautiful—
who can keep them as they are?
Unceasingly in their faces
the life in them arises and goes forth.
Like dew from morning grass,
like steam from a plate of food,
what is ours goes out from us.

Where does a smile go, or the upward glance,
the sudden warm movement of the heart?
Yet that is what we are. Does the universe
we dissolve into
taste of us a little?

From the Second Duino Elegy

———∞∞∞———

No Miracles, Please

I would rather sense you
as the earth senses you.
In my ripening
ripens
what you are.

No miracles, please.
Just let your laws
become clearer
from generation to generation.

From The Book of Hours II, 15

Autumn Day

Lord, the time has come. Summer was abundant.
Cast your shadows over the sundial,
across the fields unleash your winds.

Command the final fruits to ripen.
Grant them two more southern days,
bring them to fullness and press
their last sweetness into the heavy wine.

Who now has no house will not build one.
Who now is alone will remain alone,
will read into the night, write long letters,
and, restless, wander streets
where leaves are blowing.

Book of Images

—∞∞—

A New Morning

And today, once again, a new morning: bright, with close, rounded clouds that frame expanses of the immeasurably deep sky. Agitation in the treetops. In everything else, restfulness. Windfall of apples. The grass softly invites you to walk out of the house. The dimness inside is alive with lights on antique silver, and their reflections in the looking glass confuse the eye as to what is enclosed within the mirror's frame.

There are so many days here, none like any other. And beneath all their differences is this great similarity: the gratitude in which they are received.

Early Journals

———∞∞∞———

Premonition

Like a flag, I am surrounded by distances.
I sense the winds that are coming
and must live them
while the things below do not yet stir.
Doors still close gently
and windows don't shake.
Ashes lie heavy on the hearth.

But I know about gales
and I shudder like the sea.
I unfurl myself and fold in again
and flail back and forth,
all alone in the great storm.

Book of Images

Saint Francis of Assisi

Where is he, the clear one
whose song has died away?
Do the poor, who can only wait,
feel that young and joyous one among them?

Does he rise for them, perhaps at nightfall—
poverty's evening star?

The Book of Hours III, 34

Il Poverello

Where is he now, who leaving wealth behind
grew so bold in poverty
that he threw off his clothes before the bishop
and stood naked in the square?

The most inward and loving of all,
he came forth like a new beginning,
the brown-robed brother of your nightingales,
with his wonder and good will
and delight in Earth.

The Book of Hours III, 33

Every Turning

Every turning of the world
knows some who are disinherited, to whom
neither the past nor the future belongs.
Even what is about to happen is still remote to them.

We should not be confused by this, but strengthened in our resolve
to preserve the still-recognizable forms.
In the middle of history, amidst all that annihilates
and the not-knowing whither, they stood
as if they had a right to be there,
under the stars of the constant heavens.

From the Seventh Duino Elegy

Train Yourself to This

You carry within you the capacity to imagine and give shape to your world. It is a pure and blessed way of living. Train yourself to this, but also trust whatever comes. If it comes from your desire, from some inner need, accept that and hate nothing.

Worpswede, July 16, 1903
Letters to a Young Poet

As If God Had Been Lost

Ask yourself, dear Mr. Kappus, if you really have lost God. Is it not rather the case that you have never yet possessed him? When would that have taken place? . . . Do you imagine that someone who really had him could lose him like a little stone, or that one who possessed him could ever be lost by him? And if you are terrified that he does not exist, at this very moment we speak of him, what reason do you have, if he never existed, for missing him and seeking him as if he had been lost?

Rome, December 23, 1903
Letters to a Young Poet

We Stand in Your Garden

Lord, we are more wretched than the animals
who do their deaths once and for all,
for we are never finished with our not dying.

Dying is strange and hard
if it is not our death, but a death
that takes us by storm, when we've ripened none within us.

We stand in your garden year after year.
We are trees for yielding a sweet death.
But fearful, we wither before the harvest.

The Book of Hours III, 8

Our Oldest Friends

Our oldest friends—the great gods
who never tried to woo us—
shall we reject them because our tools of steel
do not need them? Or shall we seek them on a map?

Those powerful friends, who receive our dead,
play no part in our wheels and gears.
We have moved our banquets far from them,
and pass their messengers with such speed

we can't hear what they say. Lonelier now,
having no one but each other, not knowing each other,
we no longer meander on curving paths, but race straight ahead.

Only in the mills do the once sacred fires still burn,
lifting ever heavier hammers, while we
diminish in strength, like swimmers at sea.

Sonnets to Orpheus I, 24

Portrait of My Father
as a Young Man

In the eyes, dream. The brow bearing witness
to something far off. About the mouth,
abundant youth, an unsmiling seductiveness.
And across the ornamental braiding
of the slender, elite uniform,
the saber's hilt and both hands
waiting quietly, driven toward nothing.
Now they are barely visible, as if they,
reaching for the Distant, were the first to disappear.
All else is veiled in its own mystery,
dissolved in its own depths.

You swiftly fading daguerreotype
in my more slowly fading hands.

New Poems

When I Go Toward You

I don't want to think a place for you.
Speak to me from everywhere.
Your Gospel can be comprehended
without looking for its source.

When I go toward you
it is with my whole life.

From The Book of Hours I, 51

The Mercy We Long For

Don't boast, you judges, that you no longer torture
or clamp an iron collar 'round the neck.
Though the mercy we long for
may rearrange your features

and the scaffold fall into disuse
like an outgrown toy,
no one is better off.
The god of true mercy would step differently

into the undefended heart.
He would enter with radiance
the way gods do, strong as the sea wind

for treasure-bearing ships, and claim us as lightly
as the child of an infinite union
absorbed in play.

Sonnet to Orpheus II, 9

—∞∞∞—

The Open

With their whole gaze
animals behold the Open.
Only our eyes
are as though reversed
and set like traps around us,
keeping us inside.
That there is something out there
we know only from the creatures' countenance.

We turn even the young child around,
making her look backward
at the forms we create,
not outward into the Open.

From the Eighth Duino Elegy

—∞∞∞—

Leaving Paradise

Be our refuge from the wrath
that drove us out of Paradise.

Be our shepherd, but never call us—
we can't bear to know what's ahead.

From The Book of Hours I, 44

In a Foreign Park

Two paths appear. They open to no one.
But sometimes, as you face them,
one allows you to proceed.
Then you think you've lost your way,
but suddenly there you are in that inner garden,
left alone again with the carved stone

and reading it again:
Baroness Britta Sophie—and once again
tracing with your finger
the time-worn number of the year.
Why does this discovery never grow faint?

What makes you stop here
just the way you did before,
as though you expected something
in this damp, untrodden place
shadowed by elms?

New Poems

———◦≈≈◦———

The Work Being
Accomplished Within You

So don't be frightened, dear friend, if a sadness confronts you larger than any you have ever known, casting its shadow over all you do. You must think that something is happening within you, and remember that life has not forgotten you; it holds you in its hand and will not let you fall. Why would you want to exclude from your life any uneasiness, any pain, any depression, since you don't know what work they are accomplishing within you?

Borgeby gärd, Sweden, August 12, 1904
Letters to a Young Poet

On Security

Outside of poetry and art, security is only and ever achieved at the cost of the most inescapable limitation. This diminishment consists of choosing to be satisfied and pleasured by a world where everything is known and where preoccupation with self is both possible and useful. But how could we want that? Our security must become a relationship to the whole, omitting nothing.

Letter to Ilse Erdman
October 9, 1916

Afterlife

I don't care for the Christian concept of an afterlife. I distance myself from it ever more, without of course taking the trouble to attack it. It may have its value, alongside so many other metaphysical hypotheses. But for me the danger is that it not only renders what is mortal more vague and inaccessible, but also—because of our longing for the Beyond—it makes us less present and earthy. As long as we are here, and cousin to tree, flower, soil, may all that is near at hand be real to us and enter fully our awareness.

Letter to Countess Margot Sizzo-Noris-Crouy

The Machine

The Machine endangers all we have made.
We allow it to rule instead of obey.
To build the house, cut the stone sharp and fast:
the carver's hand takes too long to feel its way.

The Machine never hesitates, or we might escape
and its factories subside into silence.
It thinks it's alive and does everything better.
With equal resolve it creates and destroys.

But life holds mystery for us yet. In a hundred places
we can still sense the source: a play of pure powers
that—when you feel it—brings you to your knees.

There are yet words that come near to the unsayable,
and, from crumbling stones, a new music
to make a sacred dwelling in a place we cannot own.

Sonnets to Orpheus II, 10

The Depths of His Own Being

Only someone who is ready for everything, who excludes nothing, even the most incomprehensible, will live the relationship with another as something alive and will sound the depths of his own being.

Borgeby gärd, Sweden, August 12, 1904
Letters to a Young Poet

To Give Ourselves Fully

We do not have to build a church. Let us be complete in ourselves. Let us drink ourselves empty, give ourselves fully, extend ourselves outward—until, at last, the waving treetops are our own gestures and our laughter is resurrected in the children who play beneath them. . . .

Early Journals

Autumn

Leaves are falling, falling as if from afar,
as if, far off in the heavens, gardens were wilting.
And as they fall, their gestures say "it's over."

In the night the heavy Earth is falling
from out of all the stars into loneliness.

We all are falling. This hand here is falling.
Just look: it is in all of us.

Yet there is one who holds this falling
with infinite tenderness in her hands.

Book of Images

Here Is the Time for Telling

Here is the time for telling. Here is its home.
Speak and make known: More and more
the things we could experience
are lost to us, banished by our failure
to imagine them.
Old definitions, which once
set limits to our living,
break apart like dried crusts.

From the Ninth Duino Elegy

The Moon

The way that body, the moon, sublime, purposeful,
suddenly steps out over the peak,
bringing the night to serene completion.
Just so my voice rises purely
over the mountains of No More.
And the astonished places you inhabited and left
ache more clearly for you.

Uncollected Poems

Bell

Sound, no longer defined
by our hearing. As though the tone
that encircles us
were space itself expanding.

Uncollected Poems

Too Vast to Be Contained

We may yearn to come to rest
in some small piece of pure humanity,
a strip of orchard between river and rock.
But our heart is too vast to be contained there.
We can no longer seek it in a place
or even in the image of a god or an angel.

From the Second Duino Elegy

❈

Valais

Now, the landscape of this region called Valais is indescribable. Why isn't it named when people count up the wonders of the world? At first I did not really see it, because I was comparing it in my mind with the most meaningful of my memories: with Spain, with Provence (to which, in reality, thanks to the Rhone, it is a blood relative). But now that I have learned to behold it fully on its own terms, it reveals its true dimensions to me, and I come more and more to recognize the sweetness of its character and sense the most urgent of its messages. . . . Perhaps that is reflected in a strange, inexpressible fear that I might die somewhere else before I have grasped this and taken it into myself.

Early Journals

To Meet and Be Met

I feel it now: there's a power in me
to grasp and give shape to the world.

I know nothing has ever been real
without my beholding it.
All becoming has needed me.
My looking ripens things
and they come toward me, to meet and be met.

From The Book of Hours I, 1

—∞∞∞—

Our Invisible Property

The experience and inclination and affection we put into familiar things cannot be replaced. We are perhaps the last who still will have known such things. On us is the responsibility not only to remember them, but to know their value.

The earth has no other recourse but to become invisible in us, who belong in part to what is invisible; and our own invisible property can increase during our span here.

Letter to Witold Hulewicz
November 13, 1925

Endlessly Offered into Life

Oh, the pleasure of it, always emerging new
from the loosened clay. Those who dared to come first
had hardly any help. Nevertheless cities arose
on sun-favored coasts, and pitchers filled with water and oil.

Gods: we picture them first in wild brushstrokes
which petty Fate keeps wiping away.
But gods don't die. Let us listen to them;
they will be there to hear us at the end.

We are one generation through thousands of years,
mothers and fathers shaped by children to come,
who, in their turn, will overtake them.

We are endlessly offered into life: all time is ours.
And what any one of us might be worth,
death alone knows—and does not tell.

Sonnets to Orpheus II, 24

────❦────

Between the Stars

How far it is between the stars, how much farther
is what's right here. The distance, for example,
between a child and one who walks by—
oh, how inconceivably far.

Not only in measurable spans does Fate
move through our lives.
Think how great the distance between a young girl
and the boy she avoids and loves.

Everything is far, nowhere does the circle close.
See, on the plate upon the festive table
how strangely the fish is staring.

Fish are mute, we used to think. Who knows?
We may, in the end, find that their silence
says more to us than our words.

Sonnets to Orpheus II, 10

―⦿―

What I Want

You see, I want a lot.
Maybe I want it all:
the darkness of each endless fall,
the shimmering light of each ascent.

The Book of Hours I, 14

Mohammed's Calling

When into the hidden cave the angel stepped—
he was unmistakable, so towering and radiant—
the lone man there shed all claims
and asked only to be permitted
to remain the simple man he was,
a merchant confused by his travels.
He could not read—and now a word like this
was too much for even a wise one.

But the angel, imperious, pointed over and over
to what was written on the page he held,
and would not yield and kept insisting: read.

Then the man read, and when he did the angel bowed.
It was as if he had always been reading,
and now was able to obey and bring to pass.

New Poems

Offering What We Are

Oh, the places we would pour ourselves over,
pushing into the meager surfaces
all the impulses of our heart, our desire, our need.
To whom in the end do we offer ourselves?

To the stranger, who misunderstands us,
to the other, whom we never found,
to the servant, who could not free us,
to the winds of spring, which we could not hold,
and to silence, so easy to lose.

Uncollected Poems

God Is Ripening

When gold is in the mountain
and we've ravaged the depths
till we've given up digging,

it will be brought forth into day
by the river that mines
the silences of stone.

Even when we don't desire it,
God is ripening.

The Book of Hours I, 16

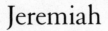

Jeremiah

Once I was as yielding as early wheat,
but it pleased you, raging one,
to ignite the heart I offered you.
Now, like a lion's, it is on fire.

What sort of mouth did you allot me,
back then when I arrived?
It was like a wound, which now is bleeding
one catastrophe after another.

Daily I resound with fresh horrors
that you, insatiable one, contrive,
and they do not destroy my mouth.
Even you lack the power to silence it now,

when those whom my people have crushed and scattered
    are finally lost.
Amidst the rubble, I would want
to keep on hearing the voice that has been mine,
from the beginning a howl.

New Poems

———∞———

Only Love Can Grasp Them

Works of art belong immeasurably to themselves, and are accessible least of all to criticism. Only love can grasp them and hold them and respond to them fairly. Always trust your own feeling, rather than others' discussions, interpretations, and arguments. Should you be mistaken, then slowly and with time the natural growth of your inner life will bring you to fuller awareness.

Viareggio, April 23, 1903
Letters to a Young Poet

———∞∞∞———

Night

Night. You with your depth-dissolving face
pressed against my face.
You, counterbalance
to my awestruck gaze.

Night, shuddering in my regard,
but in yourself so steady;
inexhaustible creation, enduring beyond
the fate of earth;

brimming with new stars, who fling
fire from their birth
into the soundless adventure
of galactic spaces:

your sheer existence,
you transcender of all things, makes me so small.
Yet, one with the darkening earth,
I dare to be in you.

Uncollected Poems

Arriving at Rodin's Place in Meudon

He has received me, but that means nothing until I tell you how. Thus: the way a beloved place receives you on your return through many tangled trails. A spring which you sang and lived for day and night while you were gone. A grove over whose leafy canopies the birds cast shadows as they fly back and forth. A path along the roses that never ceased to lead you where you needed to go. And like a great dog did he receive me, recognizing me with peaceable, caressing eyes. And like an eastern god, moving only from within his noble calm, and with the smiles of a woman and the eager hands of a child. And he led me around to see the gardens and houses and studios.

Letter to Clara Westhoff Rilke
September 15, 1905

Elegy to Marina Tsvetayeva-Efrom (II)

Oh the losses in the universe, Marina, the perishing stars!
We don't increase their number when we plunge.
In the All, everything has long been counted.
Our own falling does not diminish the sacred number.
Accepting this, we fall to the Source and heal. . . .

Waves, Marina, we are the ocean! Depths, Marina, we are the sky!
Earth, Marina, we are earth, a thousand times spring.
We are larks whose outbursts of song
fling them to the heavens.

Uncollected Poems

—∞∞∞—

Three Sprigs of Heather

Never has heather so touched and even moved me as when I found these three sprigs in your dear letter. Since then they lie in the pages of my Book of Images and permeate them with their strong, serious fragrance which is actually only the scent of autumnal Earth. And how marvelous is this scent. Never, it seems to me, has Earth so let herself be inhaled in one single fragrance. The ripe Earth, in one fragrance that is no less intense than that of the sea: bitter if you could taste it and more like honey if you could hear it. Such depths in it, of darkness, almost of the grave, and yet again wind, tar and turpentine and Ceylon tea. Serious and destitute like a beggar-monk, while also like the most precious incense, hearty and resinous. And to behold it: these sprigs of heather are like most elegant embroidery—with the violet-hued silk (a violet so moist it could be the sun's complementary color) stitching cypresses in a Persian carpet. You had to have seen that. I think that the little sprigs could not have been so lovely before you put them in your letter. You must have told them something amazing.

Letter to Clara Westhoff Rilke
September 13, 1907

~&~

The Voices

The rich and the happy can choose to keep silent,
no need to bid for attention.
But the desperate must reveal themselves,
must say: I am blind
or: I am going blind
or: It's not good for me here on Earth
or: My child is sick
or: I am not holding it together . . .

But when is that really enough?
So, lest people pass them by like objects,
sometimes they sing.

And sometimes their songs are beautiful.

Book of Images

Song of the Beggar

You'll find me in all weathers beyond the gate,
unsheltered from rain and sun.
Every so often I cradle my right ear
in my right hand.
Then my own voice sounds to me
as no one ever hears it.

Then I can't tell for certain
who is screaming:
me or someone else.
Poets cry out for more important matters.

At times I even close my eyes
so my face can disappear.
The way it lies with its full weight in my hands,
it is almost like rest.
Then no one will think I lack a place
to lay my head.

New Poems

Song of the Drunkard

It was not always with me. It would come and go.
I wanted to hold it. The wine held it for me.
What it was, I no longer know.
But I was the one being held, held this way and that,
until I could do nothing else.
I, fool.

Now I am trapped in his game,
dealt out with contempt, to be lost
over and over again to brutish death.
Each time death wins, he uses me,
a filthy card, to scratch his grey scabs,
before tossing me on the dung heap.

Book of Images

Onto a Vast Plain

Summer was like your house: you know
where each thing stood.
Now you must go out into your heart
as onto a vast plain. Now
the immense loneliness begins.

The days go numb, the wind
sucks the world from your senses like withered leaves.

Through the empty branches the sky remains.
It is what you have.
Be earth now, and evensong.
Be the ground lying under that sky.
Be modest now, like a thing
ripened until it is real,
so that he who began it all
can feel you when he reaches for you.

From The Book of Hours II, 1

Not Caught in the Drama

I can still only think of God as the One who allows everything, the One who is not caught up in the whole inexhaustible drama.

Letter to Marianne von Goldschmidt-Rothschild
December 5, 1914

Orpheus, Do You Hear?

Orpheus, do you hear
the new sound,
droning and roaring?
Many now exult in it.

Though the Machine
insists on our praise,
who can listen
with all this noise?

See, it rolls over everything,
weakening us
and taking our place.

Since its strength is of our making,
why can't it serve
and not possess us?

Sonnets to Orpheus I, 18

—∞—

Lament

How far from us everything is,
and long gone.
I think the star whose light
reaches me now
has been dead for thousands of years.

I think I heard
in the boat that went by
something anxious being said.

In a house, a clock
has struck the hour . . .
In which house?
I would like to go out from my heart
and stand under the great sky.
I would like to pray.
One of all those stars
must surely still live.

I think I used to know
which star may have kept on shining—
which one, like a white city,
rises still at the far end of its light.

Book of Images

———⊗⊗⊗———

Spectators

And we: always and everywhere spectators,
turned not toward the Open
but to the stuff of our lives.
It drowns us. We set it in order.
It falls apart. We order it again
and fall apart ourselves.

Who has turned us around like this?
Whatever we do, we are in the posture
of one who is about to depart.
Like a person lingering
for a moment on the last hill
where he can see his whole valley—
that is how we live, forever
taking our leave.

From the Eighth Duino Elegy

— ∞ —

Paintings

I am most struck by the small paintings you sent. I experience in them your old form, in miniature, where vast inner space is mirrored, where even winter and snow (and we have our share of both!) bespeak huge distance and wandering, the freshness and joy of pure undiluted youth.

Letters to Countess Margot Sizzo-Noris-Crouy
April 12, 1922

Autumn Tree

Oh tall tree of our knowing, shedding its leaves:
It's a matter now of facing the preponderance
of sky appearing through its branches.
Filled by summer, it seemed deep and thick,
filling our minds, too, so comfortably.
Now its whole interior is an avenue of stars.
And the stars do not know us.

Uncollected Poems

Pont du Carousel

The blind man who stands on the bridge
is a milestone marking the edge of the nameless.
He is the unchanging thing
around which the heavens turn,
the motionless midpoint of the stars.
All else is hurry and display.

He is the upright and unmoving one
set down amidst entangled paths.
In a heedless generation
he is a dark doorway to the underworld.

Book of Images

Friends

Friends can only be compared to dance and music. You cannot approach them intentionally, but only out of some involuntary need.

Friends must be the ends and not the means. Otherwise they can get in the way.

Early Journals

When Time Stops

In the fading forest a bird call sounds.
How out of place in a fading forest.
And yet the bird call roundly rests
in this moment that it made,
as wide as the sky above the fading forest.

All things sound together in that cry:
the whole land seems to lie within it,
the great wind seems to rest within it,
and the moment, which wants to persist,
stops, still, as if knowing things
arising from that cry
that you would have to die to know.

Book of Images

Enter Death (I)

We know nothing of this going.
It excludes us. Faced with death,
what cause have we to respond
with the fear and grief or even hatred

that twist the features to a mask of tragedy?
On this side of death we play roles.
So long as we seek to please the audience,
death, who needs no approval, plays us.

New Poems

Enter Death (II)

When you died, there broke across the stage,
through the gash your leaving made,
a shaft of reality: green of real green,
real sunlight, real trees.

Still we keep acting: fearful and solemn,
reciting our script, taking on gestures.
But you, who have been withdrawn from us,
subtracted from our very being,

now and again you overcome us,
showing us the reality we glimpsed,
so that for a while, jolted back, we are life
with no thought of applause.

New Poems

The Care in a Human Gesture

Haven't you been moved, in those early Greek carvings,
by the care you see in human gesture?
Weren't love and loss so gently laid upon the shoulders
that people seemed made of different stuff
than in our day?

Think of the hands, how they touch without pressure,
although there is strength in the torso.
These figures seem to know,
"We have come this far.
This is given to us, to touch
each other in this way.
The gods may lean on us more strongly,
but it is their nature."

From the Second Duino Elegy

———⊗∞⊗———

The Homeless Ones

There's also this to see: They will live on, they will increase,
no longer pawns of time.
They will grow like the sweet wild berries
the forest ripens as its treasure.

Then blessed are those who never turned away
and blessed are those who stood quietly in the rain.
Theirs shall be the harvest; for them the fruits.

They will outlast the pomp and power,
whose meaning and structures will crumble.
When all else is exhausted and bled of purpose,
they will lift their hands, that have survived.

The Book of Hours III, 28

All Creation Holds Its Breath

All creation holds its breath, listening within me,
because, to hear you, I keep silent.

At my senses' horizon
you appear hesitantly,
like scattered islands.

Yet standing here, peering out,
I'm all the time seen by you.

From The Book of Hours I, 18

The Things I Am

I would describe myself
like a landscape I've studied
at length, in detail;
like a word I'm coming to understand;
like a pitcher I pour from at mealtime;
like my mother's face;
like a ship that carried me
when the waters raged.

From The Book of Hours I, 13

Let This Darkness
Be a Bell Tower

Quiet friend who has come so far,
feel how your breathing makes more space around you.
Let this darkness be a bell tower
and you the bell. As you ring,

what batters you becomes your strength.
Move back and forth into the change.
What is it like, such intensity of pain?
If the drink is bitter, turn yourself to wine.

In this uncontainable night,
be the mystery at the crossroads of your senses,
the meaning discovered there.

And if the world has ceased to hear you,
say to the silent earth: I flow.
To the rushing water, speak: I am.

Sonnets to Orpheus II, 29

In Your Sight

I want to unfold.
Let no place in me hold itself closed,
for where I am closed, I am false.
I want to stay clear in your sight.

The Book of Hours I, 13

For the Animals

For the animals their death
is, as it were, completed.

What's ahead is God.
And when they move,

they move in timelessness,
as fountains do.

From the Eighth Duino Elegy

—∞∞∞—

Two Solitudes Protecting
Each Other

The experience of loving, that now disappoints so many, can actually change and be transformed from the ground up into the building of a relationship between two human beings, not just a man and a woman. And this more authentic love will be evident in the utterly considerate, gentle, and clear manner of its binding and releasing. It will resemble what we now struggle to prepare: the love that consists of two solitudes which border, protect, and greet each other.

Rome, May 14, 1904
Letters to a Young Poet

Both a Breath and a Shout

I want to praise him.
Loud as a trumpet
in the vanguard of an army,
I will run ahead and proclaim.

My words will be sweet to hear.
My people will drink them in like wine
and not get drunk.

And on moonless nights, when few remain
around my tent, I will make music as soft
as a last warm wind that hovers
late and tender before the winter's chill.

So my voice becomes both a breath and a shout.
One prepares the way, the other
surrounds my loneliness with angels.

The Book of Hours III, 11

———∞∞∞———

Parting

I have felt what it is to part.
I know it still: a dark, invincible
cruel something, which reveals again
the depth of our bond, and tears it in two.

How unguarded I was as I faced it.
I felt you pulling me and letting me go,
while staying behind, merging with all women,
becoming nothing more than this:

a waving hand, no longer intended for me alone;
a waving that continues and grows indistinct.
Perhaps a blossoming plum tree
from which a bird has just taken flight.

New Poems

—∞∞∞—

The Life Being Lived

And yet, though we strain
against the deadening grip
of daily necessity,
I sense there is this mystery:

All life is being lived.

Who is living it, then?
Is it the things themselves,
or something waiting inside them,
like an unplayed melody in a flute?

Is it the winds blowing over the waters?
Is it the branches that signal to each other?

Is it flowers
interweaving their fragrances,
or streets, as they wind through time?

Is it the animals, warmly moving,
or the birds, that suddenly rise up?

Who lives it, then? God, are you the one
who is living life?

The Book of Hours II, 12

Like a Flower I Knew

It's you, dear Vera, I would remember now,
like a flower I knew before I could name it.
I would show you to the gods,
you vanished one, you unforgotten cry.

Dancer before all else, you hesitated,
paused, as if your youth could be cast in bronze.
Bringing grief and a strange attention,
your music changed the heart.

Then the illness came. Shadows gathered,
a darkness in the blood,
cutting short your springtime.

And, as if your dancing
were a knocking at the door,
it opened, and you entered.

Sonnets to Orpheus I, 25

Were You Not Always Distracted

Were you not always distracted by yearning,
as though some lover were about to appear?

Let yourself feel it, that yearning.
It connects you with those
who have sung it through the ages,
sung especially of love unrequited.
Shouldn't this oldest of sufferings
finally bear fruit for us?

From the First Duino Elegy

The Island of the Sirens

When his hosts would ask him late in the evening
to tell of his voyages and the perils they brought,
the words came easily enough,
but he never knew

just how to convey the fear and with what startling
language to let them perceive, as he had,
that distant island turn to gold
across the blue and sudden stillness of the sea.

The sight of it announces a menace
different from the storm and fury
which had always signaled danger.
Silently it casts its spell upon the sailors.

They know that on that golden island
there is sometimes a singing—
and they lean on their oars, like blind men,
as though imprisoned

by the stillness. That quiet contains
all that is. It enters the ear
as if it were the other side
of the singing that no one resists.

New Poems

—∞—

The Sybil

They called her old even long ago.
But she kept living on, coming down the same street
day after day. They began to reckon
her age in centuries, the way they do with forests.

There she was every evening,
standing in the same place
like the tower of a ruined fortress,
unbent and hollowed out by fire.

Words that, against her will,
swarmed within her,
now fly around her, shrieking,
while others that she still holds back,
lurk in the caverns of her eyes,
waiting for night.

New Poems

—∞—

A Woman Going Blind

She sat quite like the others, having tea.
She seemed, I noted, to hold her cup
somewhat differently from the others.
She smiled once. It almost hurt to see.

When everyone stood at the end and moved about,
chatting and laughing, and as it happened,
drifting through the rooms of the house,
I watched her. She followed after,

holding back a little, as if she feared
to draw attention to herself.
On her eyes, bright with happiness,
light shone as on the surface of a pond.

She moved at her own pace and took her time
as though there were something yet to be learned:
some threshold, which once she crossed over,
she would no longer feel her way, but fly.

New Poems

All Will Come Again
into Its Strength

All will come again into its strength:
the fields undivided, the waters undammed,
the trees towering and the walls built low.
And in the valleys, people as strong
and varied as the land.
And no churches where God
is imprisoned and lamented
like a trapped and wounded animal.

From The Book of Hours II, 25

———∞∞∞———

Echoing the Ocean's Vastness

The silence must be immense where you are living right now, immense enough to allow such tumult of sound and motion. And if you think that in the ocean's vastness there exists not only the present moment but reverberations of primordial harmonies, then you can be patient and trust the great and indelible solitude at work in you. This will be a nameless influence in all that lies ahead for you to experience and accomplish, rather as if the blood of our ancestors moves in us and combines with ours in the unique, unrepeatable being that at every turn of our life we are.

Paris, December 26, 1908
Letter to a Young Poet

—∞—

The Capacity to Be Alone

Could there be a solitude that had no value to it? There is only one solitude; it is vast and hard to bear. How often do we gladly exchange it for any kind of sociability, however trivial and cheap, or trade it for the appearance of agreement, however small, with the first person who comes along. But those may be the very moments when your solitude can grow; its growing is painful as the growing of boys and sad as the beginning of spring. But don't be confused. All that is needed is the capacity to be alone with yourself, to go into yourself and meet no one for hours—that is what you need to achieve. To be alone, the way you were as a child, when the grown-ups walked around so busy and distracted by matters that seemed important because they were beyond your comprehension.

Rome, December 23, 1903
Letters to a Young Poet

The Ancient One

At the bottom,
the ancient one,
tangled root of all that has been,
forgotten fountain left unseen.

Helmets and hunters' horns,
old men muttering,
brothers betrayed,
women played upon.

Branch thrusts upon branch,
nowhere a free one.
Yes, up there! Keep climbing!

See if they'll hold you.
That high one bends already
to become a lyre.

Sonnets to Orpheus I, 17

———∞———

Along with the Laughter

Lovers.
Awakening desire,
make a place where pain can enter.
That's how we grow.

Along with their laughter,
lovers bring suffering
and longings that had slept and now awaken
to weep in a stranger's arms.

From The Book of Hours II, 10

—∞∞∞—

Autumn's End

I have seen for some time
how everything changes.
There is that which arises and acts,
kills and causes grief.

Each time I look at them
the gardens are different—
a slow decay
from gold to brown.
How long for me the way has been.

Now it is empty where I stand
and look down the avenues.
Almost as far as the farthest ocean
I can see the heavy
forbidding sky.

Book of Images

Piously We Produce

Piously we produce our images of you
till they stand around you like a thousand walls.

And when our hearts would simply open,
our fervent hands hide you.

From The Book of Hours I, 4

———⚬⚬⚬———

Completion

Dear friend, now at last I can breathe. Everything is doable now. For this was huge beyond imagining. In these days and nights I bellowed as I did back then at Duino. But even after that struggle I did not dream that such a storm of heart and spirit could come over me. That I survived it! That I survived it.

Enough. It is here.

I went outside in the cold moonlight and I caressed this little chateau Muzot as though it were a living thing—the old walls that harbored me—just as Duino once did.

Let this be called: The Duino Elegies.

Letter to Anton Kippenberg
February 9, 1922

—∞∞∞—

Necessary Experiences

Two inner experiences were necessary for the creation of these books (*The Sonnets to Orpheus* and *The Duino Elegies*). One is the increasingly conscious decision to hold life open to death. The other is the spiritual imperative to present, in this wider context, the transformations of love that are not possible in a narrower circle where Death is simply excluded as The Other.

Letter to Nanny von Escher
December 22, 1923

———∞∞∞———

On The Elegies and The Sonnets

The Elegies and The Sonnets support each other reciprocally, and I see it as an endless blessing that I, with the same breath, was able to fill both sails: the small, rust-colored sail of the sonnets and the great white canvas of the Elegies.

Letter to Witold Hulewicz
November 13, 1925

Wait and Gather

Poems don't come to much when they are written too soon. One should wait and gather the feelings and flavors of a whole life, and a long life if possible, and then, just at the end, one might perhaps be able to write ten good lines. For poems are not, as people suppose, emotions—those come easily and quickly enough. They are experiences.

For the sake of one line of poetry, one must see many cities, people, and things. One must be acquainted with animals and feel how the birds fly, and know the gestures of small flowers opening at the first light. One must be able to think back on paths taken through unknown places, on unanticipated meetings, and on farewells one had long seen coming, on days of childhood not yet understood; on parents one disappointed when they offered some pleasure one could not grasp (it was a pleasure suited to another); on childhood illnesses that came on so strangely, altering everything; on days in closed and quiet rooms and on mornings by the sea; on the sea itself, on all seas; on night journeys that rose and flew with the stars. . . .

The Notebooks of Malte Laurids Brigge

For the Sake of One
Line of Poetry

. . . And to think of all these things is still not enough. One must remember many nights of love, of which none was like another. One must remember the cries of women in labor and the pale, distracted sleep of those who have just given birth and begin to close again. But one must also have been with the dying and sat beside the dead in the room with the open window and the fitful sounds of life. And it is still not enough to have memories: one must be able to forget them when they crowd the mind and one must have the immense patience to wait until they come again. For it is not the memories themselves. Only when they become our blood, our glance, our gesture, nameless and indistinguishable from who we are—only then can it happen that in a very rare hour the first word of a poem rises from their midst and goes forth.

The Notebooks of Malte Laurids Brigge

Be Comforted and Glad

Is there anything that can take from you the hope of being someday in the God you are helping to create in each attentive act of love?

Please celebrate this Christmas with the earnest faith that He may need this very anguish of yours in order to begin. These very days that are such a trial for you may well be the time when everything in you is working at Him, as once you so urgently did as a child. Be patient and without resentment, and know that the least we can do is to make His Becoming no more difficult than Earth makes it for spring when it wants to arrive. Be comforted and glad.

Rome, December 23, 1903
Letters to a Young Poet

The Double Realm

Only he who lifts his lyre
in the Underworld as well
may come back
to praising, endlessly.

Only he who has eaten
the food of the dead
will make music so clear
that even the softest tone is heard.

Though the reflection in the pool
often ripples away,
take the image within you.

Only in the double realm
do our voices carry
all they can say.

Sonnets to Orpheus I, 9

— ∞∞ —

Probe the Depths from Which Your Life Springs

My only advice for you is this. Go within yourself and probe the depths from which your life springs, and there at its source you'll find the answer to the question of whether you must write. Accept this answer, just as you hear it, without hesitation. It may be revealed that you are called to be an artist. Then take this lot upon you, and bear it, its burden and its greatness, without asking for any external reward. For the creative artist must be a world for himself, and find everything within himself—and in nature, to which he is devoted.

Paris, February 17, 1903
Letters to a Young Poet

Wheel of God

You are a wheel at which I stand,
whose dark spokes sometimes catch me up,
revolve me nearer to the center.
Then all the work I put my hand to
widens from turn to turn.

From The Book of Hours I, 45

The Poet's Epitaph

Rose, oh pure paradox, desire
to be no one's sleep beneath
the many eyelids of your petals.

Uncollected Poems
(Lines composed on October 27, 1925,
with instructions to be carved on his gravestone)

Last Thing

Come, you last thing. I recognize you,
unholy agony in the body's weave.
Just as I burned in my mind, now I burn in you.
The wood has long resisted, holding back
from the flames you ignite—
now I feed you and blaze in you.
In the grip of your rage my natural mildness
becomes a raging hell, unlike anything.
Quite pure, free of all thoughts,
I climb the twisted pyre of future suffering,
knowing now that there is nothing I can purchase
for the comfort of this heart. All its learnings now are silent.
Is it still I who burn beyond recognition?
I will not drag memories inside.
Oh Life, Life: to be outside.
I am in flames. No one who knows me.

Last entry in Rilke's last notebook,
included among his uncollected poems

December 31

The Flower of Farewell

Somewhere the flower of farewell is blooming.
Endlessly it yields its pollen, which we breathe.
Even in the breeze of this beginning hour we breathe farewell.

Uncollected Poems

Source by Book

LETTERS

January 4, January 6, January 11,
January 24, January 26, February 2,
February 27, March 28, March 29,
April 2, April 6, April 15, April 18,
April 29, May 3, May 5, May 13, June
3, June 26, June 29, July 12, July 17,
August 11, August 18, September 10,
September 15, October 18, October 19,
October 30, November 9, November 11,
November 16, November 20, December
20, December 21, December 22

LETTERS TO A YOUNG POET

January 14, January 15, January 18,
January 27, January 31, February 6,
February 18, February 20, February 21,
February 24, March 3, March 4, March
8, March 16, April 7, April 11, April 22,
April 23, May 4, May 19, May 21, May
24, May 27, May 30, May 31, June 19,
July 11, July 15, July 19, July 26, August
2, August 6, August 7, August 29,
September 8, September 9, September
27, September 28, October 7, October
8, October 17, October 21, November 7,
December 4, December 14, December
15, December 25, December 27

NEW POEMS

January 12, January 17, January 30,
February 5, February 12, February 13,
February 14, March 9, March 10, March
15, March 31, April 1, April 10, April
16, April 19, April 30, May 6, May 23,
May 25, June 5, June 6, June 8, June 13,
June 14, June 15, June 23, June 24, June
25, July 7, July 8, July 9, July 10, July 13,
July 29, August 8, August 9, August

20, August 21, September 3, September
4, September 5, September 6, September 7, September 20, September 21,
September 22, October 11, October 16,
November 3, November 6, November
13, November 25, December 2, December 6, December 10, December 11,
December 12

SONNETS TO ORPHEUS

January 13, January 16, January 19,
January 23, February 3, February 16,
February 23, February 26, March 1,
March 21, April 9, April 25, April 28,
May 1, June 16, June 17, June 18, June
21, June 27, July 5, July 31, August 19,
August 22, August 25, September 1,
October 10, October 13, October 20,
October 31, November 1, November 17,
December 1, December 8, December
16, December 26

THE NOTEBOOKS OF MALTE LAURIDS BRIGGE

December 23, December 24

UNCOLLECTED POEMS

January 2, January 7, January 10,
February 7, February 8, February 9,
February 10, March 13, April 3, April
4, April 5, April 8, April 12, April 13,
April 14, April 17, April 27, May 9,
May 10, May 17, June 4, July 1, July
3, July 30, September 13, October 25,
October 26, November 4, November 8,
November 10, November 21, December
29, December 30, December 31